On the morning of November 22, 1919, Sol Dacus, head of the newly formed union of African American sawmill workers and loggers in Bogalusa, Louisiana, site of the Great Southern Lumber Company, the world's largest lumber mill, emerged from his hiding place in the swamps and walked boldly down Columbia Street, Bogalusa's main avenue. The day before, company agents had obtained a warrant for his arrest, charging him with being a "dangerous and suspicious character." That night, he had narrowly escaped from a mob made up of company gunmen and members of the Self-Preservation and Loyalty League (SPLL), a white vigilante organization recently formed by Bogalusa's leading business and professional men. Dacus was certain that the mob had intended to lynch him. Walking on either side of him down Columbia Street were two white "comrades-in-arms," Stanley O'Rourke and J. P. Bouchillon, both carpenters and staunch union men, each carrying a shotgun. As they marched down the busy street, the white men "loudly announced" that they would protect Dacus. The three union activists then proceeded to the headquarters of Bogalusa's Central Trades and Labor Council, located at the auto repair garage run by its president, Lem Williams, and took refuge there.[1]

The sight of Dacus confidently walking beside the two white unionists enraged numerous white citizens of the town, several of whom promptly contacted Bogalusa's police, demanding that the three be arrested. The city court immediately issued arrest warrants, charging the union men with "disturbing the peace." Bogalusa's police commissioner and its commissioner of safety decided that the arrests could best be carried out by a posse of "special policemen." Agents of the Great Southern then blew the mill siren whistle, the "riot" signal that assembled a posse of company gunmen and SPLL members.[2]

Numbering about 150 men, the posse converged on Lem Williams's garage. It is unclear who fired first, but "all hell broke loose." Jules LeBlanc, an SPLL leader, was wounded in the arm. But the union men, no more than seven, were vastly outnumbered, and within minutes Lem Williams, J. P. Bouchillon, and another union carpenter, Thomas Gaines, had been shot dead by the posse, and Stanley O'Rourke had been mortally wounded. A fifth white unionist, James Williams, surrendered. But Sol Dacus, the posse's "chief quarry," escaped.[3]

Stephen H. Norwood
From "Bogalusa Burning: The War Against Biracial Unionism in the Deep South, 1919," *Journal of Southern History* 63, no. 3 (August 1997)

1. Mary White Ovington, "Bogalusa," *Liberator*, January 1920, in Box C-319, Papers of the National Association for the Advancement of Colored People (Manuscript Division, Library of Congress, Washington, D.C.)…; "Answer of J. B. Lindsley et al. to Petitions," *Mrs. L. E. Williams* v. *Great Southern Lumber Company (GSL)*, Supreme Court of the United States, October Term, 1928, No. 252, p. 48, Box 10050, Appellate Case Files, Records of the Supreme Court of the United States, Record Group 267 (National Archives, Washington, D.C.)…; and *New Orleans Times-Picayune*, April 19, 1921.

2. "Answer of J. B. Lindsley et al.," *Williams* v. *GSL*, 48, and "Opinion of the Court," April 16, 1928, *Williams* v. *GSL*, 3, both in Box 10050, RG 267.

3. "Petition," *Williams* v. *GSL*, 4, Box 10050, RG 267; Ovington, "Bogalusa"; *New Orleans Times-Picayune*, November 23, 1919; and Bogalusa *Enterprise and American*, November 27, 1919.

ROAD NEAR NEW WESTMINSTER, BRITISH COLUMBIA. DOUGLAS FIR AND GIGANTIC CEDAR.
(*From a Sketch by the Marquis of Lorne.*)

A House Divided

Only the king has eyes. The rest of us depend on sense; our troth, feelings. Hot or cold. Dry or wet. Dirt, metal, leaf—or wood. We smell fiber, time, the force within a cut of green branch. We smell the rain-soaked trunk, young oak felled by last night's lightning still thrilling the air. We know which way to go.

The back porch where you had your coffee this morning, its post sunk into soil. That old sideboard you picked at the church sale. The crack in your neighbor's slab. You think you own your property. You think your yard is separate. But our city lies underneath the lines. Some of us just fly in.

You're angry. But we are blind. We are born to scarcity, a thousand eggs a day. We are not bothered by reason or memory. We don't make plans. We find, we feed. We feed each other, we feed on each other. We feed our young on what we retch. Compulsion has no sense of consequence. To love rot is to quicken it.

But I don't have to tell you that. *Termit-. Termes. Tarmit-. Tarmes.* To bore. To pierce. To breach the bar. Intrude. You named us. You know, don't you, our countless ancient wants, wriggling through white soldier bodies, open mouths. You know treason. Look at your own thoughts, those wasting, warring, nymphs. You know, to be rid of us, you must poison your own ground.

Rebecca Gayle Howell

ST. MARY'S CHURCH.

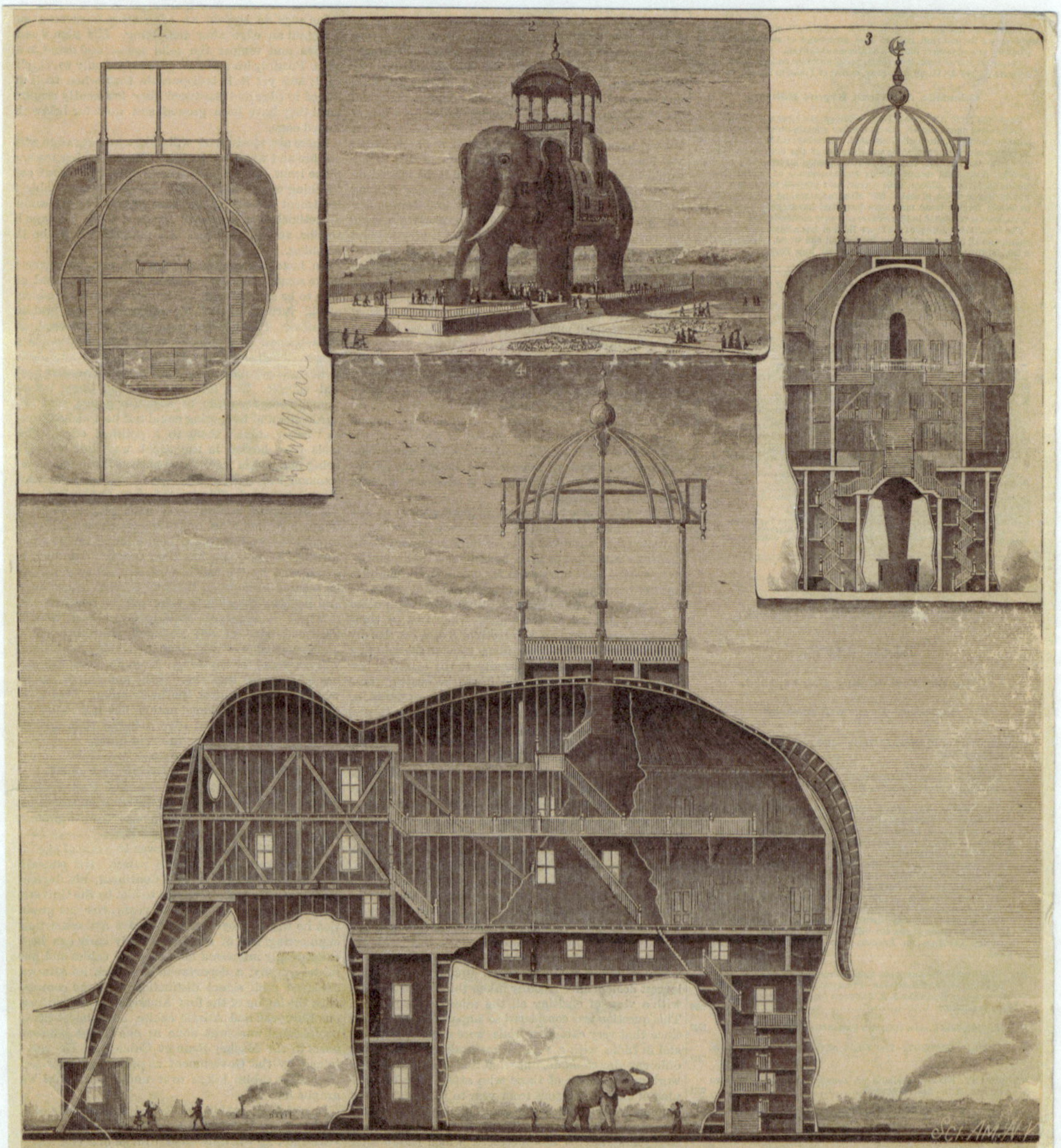

THE COLOSSAL ELEPHANT OF CONEY ISLAND.

Jason Bateman is infrastructure. In his two most famous adult roles, he is the glue holding together a family that doubles as a criminal enterprise. The opening voiceover for *Arrested Development* describes Bateman's character, Michael Bluth, as "the one son who had no choice but to keep [his family] together" in the wake of his father's criminality. In *Ozark*, Marty Byrde is both the patriarch who cost his family everything and the one struggling to keep them together after his last-ditch attempt to avoid execution by a Mexican cartel forces them to uproot their lives.

Perhaps inevitably, both shows feature wood framing. In *Arrested Development*, it is part of a series of odd, in-between structures that constantly recur—most memorably the "model home" for a failed property development where the Bluth family lives and a truck outfitted with a ladder for a repossessed private plane. The wood framing is left visible in the home's attic, where Michael's son, George Michael, is hiding his grandfather after the latter breaks out of prison. When George Michael confesses, using an affectionate nickname, that he "has Pop-Pop in the attic," Michael at first assumes he is using a euphemism for masturbation—correctly intuiting that the wood framing marks off a space of secret transgressions.

Ozark also abounds in strangely unstable infrastructure. The show's setting, Lake of the Ozarks, is itself a scheme—a valley that was flooded to draw in tourist dollars—and thus provides the perfect backdrop for Marty's increasingly baroque financial chicanery. We see wood framing in the context of one of Marty's boldest and most cynical ploys, building a church to launder money. Here again the exposed framing signals transgression, but in keeping with *Ozark*'s darker tone, the stakes are much higher: the minister and his wife are murdered and a criminal matriarch steals their baby.

Adam Kotsko

Image captions

p. 3
Alfred T. Palmer, photographer. War housing under construction in Erie, Pennsylvania, July 1941. United States Farm Security Administration, Office of War Information Photograph Collection, Library of Congress. Public domain

p. 4 top
A rendering of a tree trunk sawn into pieces of lumber, published in Almerico Ribera, *Legno, l'universo costruttivo di un materiale nuovo*, 2015. Courtesy of Almerico Ribera

p. 4 center
A performance of Rodgers and Hammerstein's *Oklahoma!* staged at Indiana University, Jacobs School of Music Opera and Ballet Theater, 2016. Set design by Steven Kemp. Photo © Steven C. Kemp

p. 4 bottom
Darius Kinsey, photographer. Logging/timber scene, negative circa 1910. Gelatin silver print, 10 15/16 × 13 9/16 in (27.8 × 34.5 cm). 84.XM.490.13, The J. Paul Getty Museum, Los Angeles. Digital image courtesy of the Getty's Open Content Program

p. 5 top
A lumber yard on the east side of Sampson's Slip, on the South Branch of the Chicago River between Loomis and Throop Streets, Chicago, July 2, 1903. Courtesy of the Metropolitan Water Reclamation District of Greater Chicago

p. 5 bottom
Lumber yards at Clark Street and the Chicago River between 12th and 14th Streets, Chicago, circa 1870. ICHi-003740, Chicago History Museum

p. 7 top
Blockhouse, Fort McKeen, Mandan, North Dakota, 1940s. The State Historical Society of North Dakota

p. 7 center
An International CO-4000 tractor truck and trailer loaded with lumber from Bunting Sawmill and Lumber, a wholesale company based in Hulmeville, Pennsylvania, 1960s. LM2018.10.6, Pennsylvania Lumber Museum, Pennsylvania Historical and Museum Commission

p. 7 bottom
Yards of the Great Southern Lumber Company, Bogalusa, Louisiana, between 1860 and 1920. Photography Collection, The New York Public Library

p. 8
Douglas firs and cedar on the road near New Westminster, British Columbia, from a sketch by the Marquis of Lorne, 1870. Mary Evans Picture Library

p. 9 top
Wood-framed buildings burning, unknown dates and locations. Courtesy of the Peter J. Cohen Collection

p. 9 bottom
Theroud, illustrator. Sawmill, California, published in *Le Tour du Monde*, 1870. The Print Collector / Alamy Stock Photo

p. 11 top
"I Heard Someone…," *Gasoline Alley*, 1934. Gasoline Alley / TCA. Image courtesy of Sunday Paper Press

p. 11 bottom left
Lewis Baltz, photographer. *Night Construction, Reno Nevada*, 1977. Gelatin silver print on Agfa paper; image 6 7/16 × 9 1/2 in (16.4 × 24.1 cm); sheet 8 × 9 15/16 in (20.3 × 25.2 cm). Gift from the Collection of Joe Deal and Betsy Ruppa, 2010.82.35.7, RISD Museum. Image courtesy of the RISD Museum, Providence, RI. © Estate of Lewis Baltz

p. 11 bottom right
Still from *E.T. the Extra-Terrestrial*, directed by Steven Spielberg, Universal Pictures, 1982. Fair use

p. 12 top
Illustration of St. Mary's Church, from A. T. Andreas, *History of Chicago*, volume 1, 1884. Public domain

p. 12 bottom
"The colossal elephant of Coney Island," published in *Scientific American*, 1885. Picture Collection, The New York Public Library

American Framing

The Same Something for Everyone

American Framing

Edited by
Paul Andersen
Jayne Kelley
Paul Preissner

PARK BOOKS

Contents

6
Excerpt from "Bogalusa Burning"
Stephen H. Norwood

10
A House Divided
Rebecca Gayle Howell

13
Jason Bateman Is Infrastructure
Adam Kotsko

21
Something Else for Everyone
Paul Andersen

27
American Hutness
Dan Handel

33
Photographs
Chris Strong

75
American Framing
Pavilion of the United States at the 17th International Architecture Exhibition – La Biennale di Venezia

153
Examples from history

177
Photographs
Daniel Shea

221
Architecture *Americana*
Penelope Dean

227
How Framing Works
Paul Preissner

232
Acknowledgements

233
Biographies

234
Imprint

237
Excerpt from "The Ancient Forest"
Catherine Caufield

245
Excerpt from "Helping the Powerless Build Power"
Pablo Alvarado, Harold Meyerson

248
Hacksaw
Ernest Wilkins

Something Else for Everyone
Paul Andersen

Wood framing is crude, thin, and cheap, and wood-framed buildings tend to be dull and conservatively designed. What do we make of these qualities?

×

Pragmatism, which emphasizes usefulness and action, is akin to natural law in the United States. In buildings, Americans go with what works, whether or not it conforms to accepted ideas of what makes architecture good. A pragmatic option that solves the problem at hand supersedes style, timelessness, opulence, idealism, and history.

As nineteenth-century settlers moved across the continent, they faced logistical problems that came with building in remote locations. They needed houses, barns, shops, forts, and other buildings, but didn't always have money, technical skill, or the means to handle heavy materials. Demand increased with the Homestead Acts, which conferred ownership of 160 acres of public land to any citizen, provided that they live on the land and improve it. Under this act, settlers claimed 270 million acres, or 10 percent of the area of the United States, and the most popular improvement method was to build a house. The dense forests of the upper Midwest provided a generous supply of softwood lumber, which could be floated down Lake Michigan to the nearly treeless prairie and carried by railroad and wagon to distant building sites. The wood was soft, but affordable, lightweight, and abundant, so settlers developed a new system of construction to make use of it. Unable to assemble robust wood frames with stiff joints—like the heavy timber construction of Germany, northern Europe, and Japan—they nailed together a thin stick frame and stiffened it with a skin of diagonal wood strips. The pragmatism behind the early development of wood framing uncoupled settlers from European traditions and allowed their buildings to be original in character and concept.

×

In framing's wild infancy, buildings took a variety of forms. Many of them looked like misfits by today's standards: round barns, houses that were part log cabin and part balloon frame, and warehouses that resembled upside-down ships, to name a few. The blockhouse—a two-story military-post building where the upper floor overhung the lower floor and was often rotated 45 degrees—was a particularly eccentric invention. The rotation was a practical solution to the problem of surveying the surrounding territory through tiny windows designed to protect people inside from enemy fire. Any one small window would provide only a narrow view out, but many windows in different locations and with different orientations would allow a group of people to collectively construct a panoramic view.

Blockhouses were common in frontier forts, especially where the US government claimed land that was inhabited by Indigenous Americans. Not long after the first forts were built, the Indian Wars ended. Disease brought and warfare waged by settlers had quickly decimated the population of Indigenous groups on the Great Plains. True to its matter-of-fact origins, the blockhouse was a dead type as soon as it no longer served a purpose, less than twenty years after it first appeared. Seeing photos of the blockhouse now, its miniature windows, misaligned floor plans, and top-heavy massing defy conventions of wood-frame building design. Even though it was originally devised to straightforwardly solve problems, it stands out more as an anachronistic example of architectural design than for any contribution to construction. The essential conditions of this wild architecture were a set of specific and uncommon functional requirements, a construction system still in an adolescent and unregulated stage of development, and a commitment to a pragmatic solution above all else.

×

Wood framing has conflicting histories. Over the years, it has embodied rugged individualism and homeowners associations, grassroots invention and industrial standardization. The design freedom that pragmatism brought to framing gradually became a constraint, narrowly limiting the variety of wood-framed buildings being built in the US. As soon as framing methods provided adequate solutions to the problems confronting builders, the most pragmatic approach became replicating those methods, not experimenting with untested ideas. Wood framing comes with conventions these days—legal codes and rote habits that dictate the sizes, shapes, quantities, and positions of building parts. For the most part, it hasn't provoked new forms or styles for generations. It has ossified, become the raw material of a predictable and homogenous building culture. Most framed buildings are steeped in tradition, even if the traditions are not particularly old.

Lots of peculiar buildings were built in the wilderness, where problems posed by the harsh context and settlers' lack of experience with stick framing led to distinctive massing, improvised composition, and unprecedented building types. They were on the fringe—of the geography and politics of the American frontier and in their indifference to deeply rooted traditions in design and construction. Resurrecting the bold independence that the 2×4 once endorsed would restore the possibility of new kinds of projects, mostly because of how architecturally stale framing itself has become.

×

Nonconformist movements in architecture usually originate in the design culture that they upend. They reject the predominant ideals of their time while using the same raw material as their predecessors. Mannerists used the basic components of classical architecture, but incorrectly, to create new aesthetic effects from the vocabulary that they inherited. Late modernists did the same, imbuing modern form with an exuberance and idiosyncrasy that purists before them had considered anathema. Similar cases can be made for Rococo, Constructivism, the ecology movement, Deconstructivism, and other movements that set out to contest the prevailing design culture.

A subversive approach to ordinary buildings, rather than high architecture, might intensify their most characteristic design conventions to undercut the moderate homogeneity that those conventions usually produce. As a result, architecture could push the predictable urban fabric of real estate development toward new visions of buildings and cities, for fun or for a purpose. Mainstream design could underwrite shifts from familiar to mysterious, from broad acceptance to selective enthusiasm, from passive reproduction to collective experimentation, and from formulaic neutrality to expressions of preference.

×

An underrated strategy—exaggerate a flaw. History is full of examples, from the bent classical facade of Palazzo Massimo alle Colonne to the rock in Albert Frey's house. The flaw is usually a site contingency or misfit building program. Michelangelo was particularly skilled at using compromised conditions to distort Renaissance compositional systems. When Pope Paul III asked him to design a piazza on Capitoline Hill, the site presented several problems. The most difficult was that the two most important existing buildings were set at an acute angle. At the time, architects preferred perpendicular alignments that simulated the space of perspective drawings. Rather than demolish and rebuild one of the existing buildings at a right angle, he added a building at the same acute angle. Doubling the improper angle created a piazza with a trapezoidal plan and an exaggerated sense of perspective. He defied a design principle that was unquestionable at the time and exceeded its intended effect.

×

Exaggeration can combine novelty and familiarity. Everyday forms and materials can embody new architectural ideas when rearranged or embellished.

Some exaggeration methods:

Quantities—none, fewer than usual, more than usual, all.
Sizes—smaller or bigger than usual; consistent or inconsistent sizes.
Proportions—significantly smaller or larger ratios.
Application—comprehensive or selective; apply changes holistically, to one part or type of part, or to one characteristic but not others.

Working off ordinary buildings suggests a model of authorship based on a found signature. Taking design conventions to extreme conclusions might produce a sensibility that is simultaneously generic and radical, anonymous and exceptional.

×

Three stories about wind…

1. Early skeptics figured that balloon-framed buildings would be flimsy. George Woodward, an architect and engineer, defended their stability in a series of articles published in 1860 in *The Cultivator*, the journal of the New York State Agricultural Society. He told the story of a balloon-framed house that blew off its foundation in heavy winds, rolled down a hill, and came to a stop completely intact.

2. L. Frank Baum begins *The Wonderful Wizard of Oz*:

    "Dorothy lived in the midst of the great Kansas prairies, with Uncle Henry, who was a farmer, and Aunt Em, who was the farmer's wife. Their house was small, for the lumber to build it had to be carried by wagon many miles."

    When the tornado hit, "the house whirled around two or three times and rose slowly through the air. Dorothy felt as if she were going up in a balloon."

    Hours later, the house landed in Oz, intact, and Dorothy and Toto walked outside.

3. Two Italian architects at the opening of La Biennale:

"These wood-frame buildings are beautiful, but don't they fall apart in tornadoes?"

Of the many unremarkable buildings, wood-framed buildings are exceptionally mediocre. As a group, they not only epitomize suburban dullness, but are architecturally poor, at least by traditional standards. Customarily, architecture should be stable, heavy, and timeless. Wood framing is lightweight and easily altered.

One way to escape framing's mediocrity is to exaggerate its flaws.

If being light is a flaw, make it lighter. A naked frame or partially clad frame. An external frame, fully exposed on the outside. An inflated envelope that expands the hollow cavities inside walls, floors, and ceilings. Studs and joists that are frames themselves.

If the flaw is thinness, make it thinner. All sheathing.

If the problem is rough materials and connections, make them rougher. Warped and pitted walls, floors, and ceilings. The most twisted, knotted, and bent lumber, nails that stick out, unfinished drywall joints.

If redundant and inefficient use of materials is a flaw, make it less efficient. Excessively copied parts.

If ad hoc organization is a constraint, make it more ad hoc. Isolated irregularities rather than a comprehensive lack of repetition. Intense instances of nonuniformity. Formalized idiosyncrasies. Oddly regular arrangements of quirks.

The artist Fred Sandback's installations—which consist of a few taut strings tracing a geometric object, like a corner or a plane—have virtually no mass. They add almost nothing to the world, but dramatically change one's impression of its banality. Sandback's first work with string, the only material that he would use for his entire career, was a thin wireframe 2×4. It was the same size as a standard 2×4, only lighter.

In late March 1845, Henry David Thoreau began building his cabin at Walden Pond. By early May, he completed the frame structure, which he made of wood from nearby pine trees. He moved in on the 4th of July, after shingling the roof and walls.

He enjoyed the thinness of his slightly clad walls so much that he put off plastering the interior until November, when the cold weather became unbearable. Without plaster, the gaps in the walls allowed him to continually breathe fresh air and feel connected to the surrounding woods. He described the experience as being less indoors than simply behind a door.

Andrew Jackson Downing, the father of American landscape architecture, published several pattern books for various sizes and types of houses. In *Cottage Residences*, published in 1842, he claimed that wood is the least desirable construction material because of its frailty. At that point in his career, he still clung to an Old World view of architecture as heavy and timeless. Thin stick framing, even if structurally stable, did not exhibit the virtues of great architecture, in his view. But he was conflicted; he knew that the light frame buildings popping up on the frontier were practical and fit to their context. So Downing proposed an American style based on pragmatism, with two notable features. One has become common: asymmetrical massing, which was intended to allow a house to respond to eccentricities in its internal planning and external site. The other was an exaggerated vertical ribbing on the exterior that matched the balloon-frame construction behind it—he doubled the structural frame and made the copy ornamental. The unusual exoskeleton created the visual impression that the house had been turned inside out, its light frame exposed.

×

Redundancy, a key factor in wood framing's structural performance, played a part in its development, too. Numerous attempts to determine who invented softwood framing have come up short. Sigfried Giedion appears to make the most definitive claim in *Space, Time, and Architecture* when he writes that George W. Snow was the inventor of the balloon frame, but then clarifies in a footnote that Snow probably does not deserve sole credit. Pinning down the first wood-framed building has been equally difficult. Several historians credit Snow's 1832 warehouse as the first; others say that it was St. Mary's Church, and that Snow built it in 1833; a third group claim that it was the church, but that Augustine Taylor designed and built it. Both buildings were located near the mouth of the Chicago River and didn't last long. Earlier accounts describe similar, but less advanced, framing methods. An 1804 deed for a piece of property in Ste. Geneviève, Missouri, describes a *maison en Boullin*, a particular type of house that the French were building along the Mississippi River. Several buildings from the same time remain and are built like typical wood framing, only the softwood studs were driven into the ground rather than being anchored to a foundation.

The origin stories of wood framing are more myth than fact. The system had no single author and did not begin with one project. It was born of a gradual and collective effort, with many anonymous inventors working across a large geographical area.

×

Skeptics of stick framing's structural integrity noted its light weight and poor material qualities. They were right about both. The lumber used for lightweight frame construction comes from pine, fir, and spruce trees, which grow fast and produce soft wood. In 1906, the Austrian wood researcher Gabriel Janka developed a method to measure the hardness of wood, which was later adopted by the American Society for Testing and Materials. The Janka test quantifies hardness as the force required to push a steel ball with a cross-sectional area of one square centimeter halfway into a wood plank. The rating for Douglas fir, the most widely used species for lumber, is 660 pounds-force. White oak, a common hardwood, has a rating of 1360, which means that more than twice as much force is needed to make the same indent in oak as in Douglas fir. Softwoods break, gouge, and splinter much more easily than the old-growth woods used in heavy timber construction. On top of that, nailed joints are notoriously weak.

Against all logic, proliferating these low-quality materials and connections can yield a sturdy structure. The key is redundancy. No one part or joint is essential. The statistical spread of nails, studs, and joists enables them to behave collectively. Like a democracy, softwood framing succeeds by consensus and distribution. Individual excellence, or failure, plays no part. The connections between wood framing and democratic principles range from symbolic to actual. Almost everybody in the US lives in a wood-framed house of the same quality. No amount of money can buy a better 2×4. And framing's irrational structural behavior—an unpredictably durable assembly of weak materials and poor connections—has both mirrored and influenced equally irrational American models of exceptionalism and equality, of the individual and the multitude.

X

Herbert Croly, an intellectual leader of the Progressive movement in the early 1900s, saw the architect as a model citizen. The architect's unique skill, Croly argued, was an ability to marshal consensus for new ideas. Being both artist and businessperson, a good architect had to balance individual excellence with popular appeal. The architect achieved the first part, excellence, by doing work that could be distinguished from their peers'. Without distinction, a prospective client would have no reason to choose them. For the second part, popular appeal, the architect needed to acquire a following, which was done socially (a small group buys in, shows their friends, a few of them join in, etc.). Excellence and appeal were mutually dependent. The more distinct the work, the more devoted its backers would be.

Croly believed that for the country to fulfill its promise of democratic opportunity, its citizens should all be excellent in some role. He forged a counterintuitive marriage of equality and originality when he envisioned a multitude of exceptional individuals, a wild mix of leader geniuses. Early wood-framed buildings anticipated a similar evolution toward collectively exceptional architecture. But the promise that an ordinary building system can birth a multitude of exceptional projects remains somewhat unfulfilled, more a project of the future than the past.

X

> Make it new.
> —Ezra Pound

> Make it plain.
> —Malcolm X

> Make it sweet again!
> —John Ashbery

American Hutness
Dan Handel

> The man is willing to make himself an abode which covers but not buries him. Some branches broken down in the forest are the proper materials for his design.[1]

This mythic account of the beginning of architecture, which opens Marc-Antoine Laugier's *Essay on Architecture*, first published in 1753, is often considered to be a universal and timeless tale of technical progress and human ingenuity. But the nameless man that makes progress is not exactly the Indigenous man of the woods; rather, he is the self-determined type shaped by the currents of the Enlightenment. In fact, he might as well have been an American.

Laugier's account fits so perfectly in the American scheme of things because it is really a tale of a solitary individualist, a utilitarian man who comes out of nowhere and constructs a shelter that becomes the origin of all architecture. What could be more pioneer in spirit? Add to that the fact that in Laugier's origin myth, the hut, meaning the individual house, is the fountainhead out of which other types of buildings emanate, and you get North American frontier settlement in a nutshell.

As a real piece of architecture, the primitive hut depends on proximity to raw material and on a certain level of processing through which this material is transformed into elemental parts to be assembled. If the hut can be recast as an American story, then proximity and processing would be its protagonists. As they change and develop, the idealized abode is layered with technical innovations and with the changing tastes of a society in perpetual flux.

×

The history of the settlement of the United States can be told through the recession of its forests: from the "green billowy sea," in John Muir's words, that supposedly predated early settlement to the Chicago lumber district that channeled the economy of the Great Plains, the emergence of a nationwide forest products economy, and the struggles of ecological forestry to undo the damage inflicted by forest corporations in the Pacific Northwest. And if the individual house made of wood is the anonymous apostle of this history, it is so not only because it represents an ideal of advancing settlement, but because it is literally made of the forest.

In quite a different account of a primitive hut, Muir described the practice of shake-makers in the Sierra Nevada in the 1880s. These men would travel light and venture deep, by themselves, into the virgin forest in order to find a spot for an abode near a meadow and a stream. They would then take down a sugar pine that seemed fit for the purpose, saw a four-foot-long section, split it, and from this first cut get "shakes enough for a cabin and its furniture,—walls, roof, door, bedstead, table, and stool." Sapling poles would make the frame of the building, and a few pounds of nails would be used to fix the shakes in place.

1 Marc-Antoine Laugier, *An Essay on Architecture* (London: T. Osborne and Shipton, 1755), 10–11.

Then the man would "[go] to work sawing and splitting for the market." The meadow would soon fill with bundles of roughly standardized shakes—four feet long, four inches wide, a quarter of an inch thick—that the man would first exchange for provisions and then advertise for sale. The primitive hut made of the forest material is the funnel through which the same material is processed and delivered to market. It becomes a micro-industrial site with a much larger environmental footprint. "Every one of the frail shake shanties," Muir notes, "is a centre of destruction, and the extent of the ravages wrought in this quiet way is in the aggregate enormous."[2]

The destructive logic that was in place in the shanties of the California forest was an unfortunate inheritance of the sawmills that dotted the banks of lakes and rivers in Michigan and Wisconsin, supplying white pine to the prairies. Around the mid-nineteenth century, frontier settlers moved for the first time from forest environments into grassland, and their demand for wood, used to build virtually everything in their communities, had to be met from a distance.[3] In the 1850s, the number of acres that were cleared of forest amounted to 40 percent of everything that was cleared in the previous two hundred years of colonization. This exploding supply enabled the boosterism that recreated the Midwest as an immense real estate draw. How far one was from a forest determined the level of processing and standardization the tree had to go through, how it traveled and was treated, how its qualities were advertised, and what species and construction method one ended up using. The ubiquitous American home was therefore far from standard: its instances were the products of an ongoing negotiation between geography, time, and market.

In the fifty years that followed the Civil War, turning nature into commodity was a central challenge for the forest industry. While certain observers were able to walk in the forests of Wisconsin and describe them as "heavily timbered,"[4] the actual transformation of stored sunshine into logs, boards, and standardized wholesale categories was far from easy. Sawmill owners and wholesalers used their own grading systems, but these proved to be too local and lacking in consistency. They then formed associations for the advancement of industry grading rules, which failed miserably as renegade mill owners stuck to their own classification methods and dealers freely manipulated grades. Only at the turn of the century was the Bureau of Grades of the Mississippi Valley Lumbermen's Association able to establish detailed grading rules enforced by inspectors and adopted by most other lumber associations, leading eventually to national standardization.[5]

However, by that time, the Age of Wood was largely over. The first decades of the twentieth century showed a constant decline in consumption of wood per capita, gradually substituted by steel, aluminum, glass, cement, and plastic products introduced to the market.[6] Lumbermen had to turn to product development and aggressive marketing. In both, the individual house was a lucrative arena for competition.

In a series of booklets published in the early 1920s, Weyerhaeuser Forest Products, one of the leading industrial lumber manufacturers to emerge out of the cutthroat era, made the case for the individual American home made of wood. For the company, the wood

---

[2]   John Muir, "The American Forests," *Atlantic Monthly*, August 1897, 154.
[3]   William Cronon, *Nature's Metropolis: Chicago and the Great West* (New York: W.W. Norton, 1991), 180.
[4]   Quoted in Cronon, 152.
[5]   Fred W. Kohlmeyer, "Lumber Distribution and Marketing in the United States," *Journal of Forest History* 27, no. 2 (April 1983): 90.
[6]   Kohlmeyer, 90.

home was the answer to the overcrowding of cities and the pitfalls of the rent system. Individual homeownership was not only a practical solution, but also about recovering an imagined past: owning one's home protected men and women against the nightmare of having "no roots or associations." Wood was the material up to the task, and Weyerhaeuser was around to help; the manufacturer hired an architect to recreate familiar architectural styles, "the foundation of American building traditions," which it then assembled in the 1922 publication *Good Houses*.[7] This conservative sales pitch masked a radical proposition, in which American Colonial- or Georgian-style homes were reconstructed in wood and adapted to the requirements of modern times. Previous centuries of building in brick and mortar were in fact but a digression from the "native tradition from the beginning of our country,"[8] which stretched from the log hut of the forefathers to the "crude shelter of squared timbers," the framed house, "with its covering of hand-wrought boards held in place by hand-wrought nails," and the present manufacture of lumber fit to the carpenter's trade. In a Darwinian argument, the author claims that the ubiquity of such examples attests to their durability, which is "so conclusively proved that we are warranted by this fact alone in building wood houses to the end of time."[9] The primitive hut is again the source of all American architecture, and the house made of wood is not only morally superior, as the title of the publication suggests, but consistent with the American way of life. It just so happened that it was also good for business.

Thus began an alliance between architects and forest products companies. Weyerhaeuser sponsored design competitions for small houses made of wood and published the winning entries, for which it made sure to acquire the rights, as model homes complete with working drawings incorporating the company's products. Other producers and several federal agencies followed, and wood-made homes were paraded into the market as both revivalist mansions and ultra-modernist prefab schemes. The vast landscape of these publications and advertisements denotes their responses to contemporary circumstances. In the 1920s tradition leads the way, whereas in the 1930s and 1940s efficiency takes the front seat. In the 1950s wood products compose and furnish suburban dream houses, and in the 1970s they enable low-cost housing for a nation wrought by economic recession. In each instance, the American wooden home is infused with changing moral, social, economic, even environmental values.

×

The appropriation of the hut by industry, with its emphasis on homogenization and standardization, was often at odds with the DIY character of American homebuilding. Even before Drop City and the *Whole Earth Catalog*, DIY was a response to a reality where everything was produced far away by someone you didn't know. It emerged as a cultural phenomenon after the Great Depression and gradually accrued psychological and social meanings. DIY manuals from the 1940s and 1950s, notes Cathy D. Smith, expose the assumption that "the construction of the family home and its interiors...involve[s] the simultaneous construction of both the individual self and the nuclear family unit."[10] Self-building

---

7   Russell Whitehead, *Good Houses: Typical Historic Architectural Styles for Modern Wood-Built Homes* (Saint Paul, MN: Weyerhaeuser Forest Products, 1922), 4.
8   The various Indigenous American traditions of home building in wood were apparently lost on the writer.
9   Whitehead, 10.
10 Cathy D. Smith, "Handymen, Hippies and Healing: Social Transformation through the DIY Movement (1940s to 1970s) in North America," *Architectural Histories* 2, no. 1 (2014), http://doi.org/10.5334/ah.bd.

was building of self—an American self, of course. In a version of Laugier's tale, a 1954 *Time* magazine article argued, "Men have puttered around since the dawn of time....And Americans, more than any other people, have always been a nation of how-toers, of putterers, tinkerers and inventors."[11] In another case, Albert Roland, a writer for the United States Information Agency, called on Thoreau to testify to the merit of garage workshops, in which men could escape the pressures of everyday capitalism and "find there a temporary *Walden*."[12]

In 1960, Herb Greene completed construction of a primitive hut in the prairie. The irregular abode was built from cedar boards and shakes that were expressively placed over a wood-sheathed two-by-six-foot frame in an "improvisational process of assembling irregular boards in a rippling collage effect."[13] This building process gave the entire thing the appearance of a slanted animal, an impression reinforced by the oculus at its upper floor. The eye room was where Julius Shulman slept for four days before making the house nationally famous with photographs that appeared in *Life* magazine. In a nod to the house's unconventional silhouette, the accompanying article compared it to a prairie chicken.[14] Greene was a student of Bruce Goff's at the University of Oklahoma, and some of the latter's organicist tendencies were quite evident in the Prairie House. Yet in building his own house Greene also pursued a deliberate roughness of forms and construction methods that responded to the standardized product that was the American home at the time.

Building one's own wooden home in the late 1950s from materials that were readily available became more complicated in most areas of the country with the increasing distances between forest resources and building sites. Lumber for construction would typically be sourced in the Pacific Northwest or the Southern states and purchased in a building materials supermarket chain store. Greene's choice of red cedar came as close as possible to the ideal of self-building with locally sourced materials, as did his hands-on collaging of planks on the outside of the building and shingling of the interior, done collectively with some of his University of Oklahoma architecture students. Unlike other primitive huts, this one articulated a cave-like interior that allowed for hyper-modernist vistas of the grassland outside. Shulman, peeking out of the eye of this strange animal of a house, supplied the visual record to these vistas and helped position Greene's hut as a renegade statement against the menace of industrial mass housing proposed in the smiling brochures of Weyerhaeuser et al.

Beyond its idiosyncrasies, the Prairie House brought up another suppressed drive of the American psyche: living off the grid. Technically, the term described homes and communities seeking disconnection from electricity and gas networks, but culturally it came to mean a conscious withdrawal from society at large, often achieved through a uniquely American cocktail of social conservatism and faith in innovative technologies. The hut was the perfect cultural relic of that sentiment, as it embodied both the qualities of pioneer spirit and nostalgia for an imagined past less contaminated by the evils of contemporary living.

---

11   "Modern Living: The Shoulder Trade," *Time*, August 2, 1954, 49.
12   Albert Roland, "Do-It-Yourself: A Walden for the Millions?," *American Quarterly* 10, no. 2 (Summer 1958): 154. Smith's text cites both Roland and *Time*.
13   Herb Greene in discussion with the author, August 14, 2020.
14   "New Homes: Wacky and Staid: A Bird, a Beast, and a Bargain," *Life*, November 24, 1961, 113.

Nostalgia and innovation are present in handful amounts in one contemporary reincarnation of American hutness and its contradictions. This is the Mastheads, in Pittsfield, Massachusetts, completed in 2017 by the architects Tessa Kelly and Chris Parkinson. The project comprises five wooden structures that can be moved around and used as open-air studios for writers participating in an annual residency program. As the wooden home ventures into the age of ecological consciousness regarding the sourcing and life expectancy of materials, cross-laminated timber (CLT) has emerged as a weapon of choice for the architecturally cultivated. In CLT, frame and panel are unified in holy matrimony, a total system of construction. The mobile huts of the Mastheads project, designed with CLT to replicate parts of the structures in which writers such as Melville or Thoreau worked, bring the notion of the wooden refuge full circle.

Iwan Baan carefully photographed the minimalist studiolos against the Berkshire woods to invoke a Waldenesque tradition. However, this backdrop was somewhat of a camouflage, as the material that made the huts was sourced in a boreal forest and shipped across the border by a wood products company from Montreal. And so New England forests were infused with dabs of Canadian timber in order to reinforce the creative potential of long-standing American intellectual and material traditions. The complexities and contradictions of these traditions were manifest, once again, in a hut.

×

Countless wooden homes pave the byways of American architecture, generously allowing propaganda of glass and steel to circulate worldwide while they remain the exception back home. In lieu of technological overkill, these abodes offer a primitiveness that is so alluring because it allows a liberty of expression, and an escape from the tyrannies of elitist tastemakers and governing bureaucrats. But this myth has long since turned into fantasy. As almost nobody lives in the forest, the act of liberation embodied in building one's home from wood gets intertwined with community ordinances, product supply chains, labor markets, and mortgage schemes.

With that, the celebrated balloon frame may become quite a weight, often one paycheck away from turning into a liability or toxic asset. The story of freedom as told in *Little House on the Prairie* or on the pages of architectural magazines is also a story of dispossession and financial subjugation for those who happen to be on the wrong side of the class and color line. As the evidence of survivalist Silicon Valley magnates spending millions on solitary bunkers in the Black Hills would attest, being free in America has turned from a natural right into a rarified commodity. But American hutness, with its massive presence and mythical origins, has at least the potential of realigning with the 99 percent and becoming an architectural vehicle for financial and cultural independency. Otherwise, its instances will remain scattered across the country as product placements for bygone individual liberties in a once democratic republic.

Photographs
Chris Strong

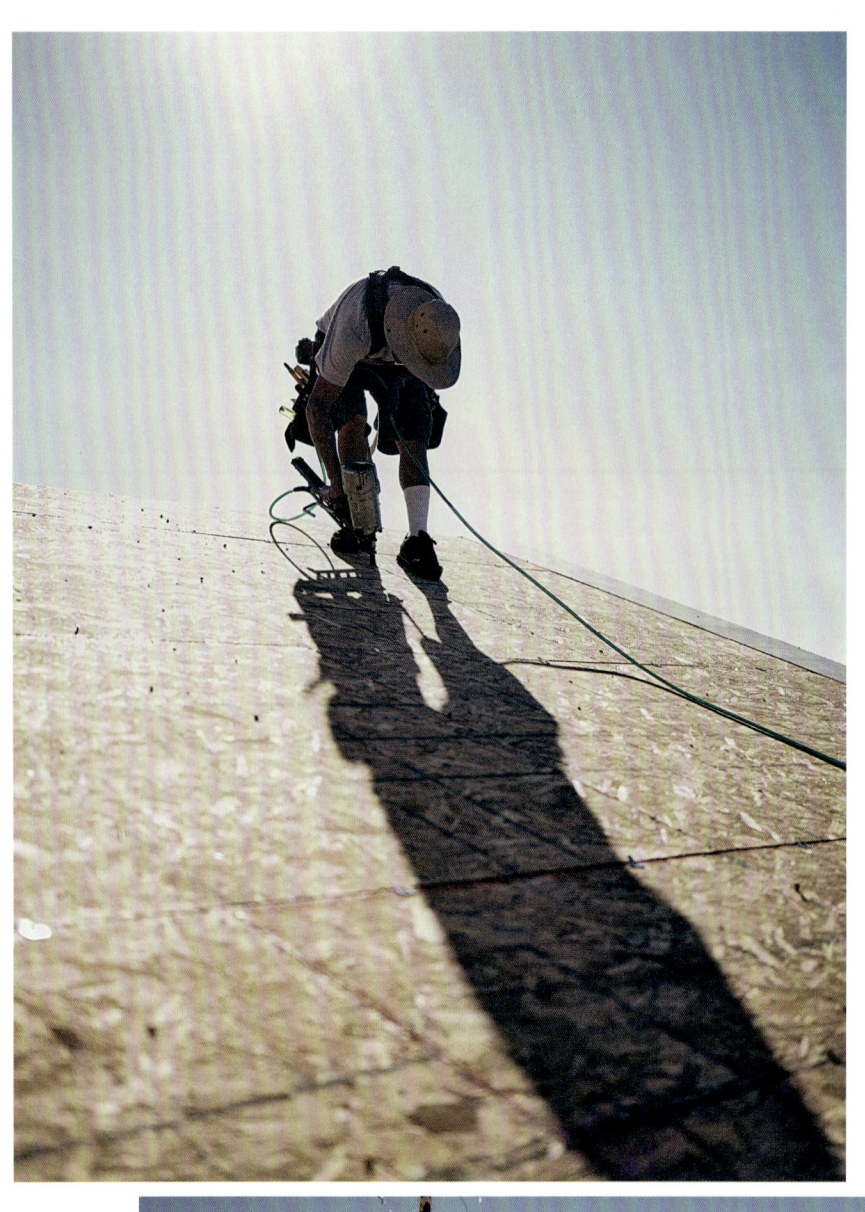

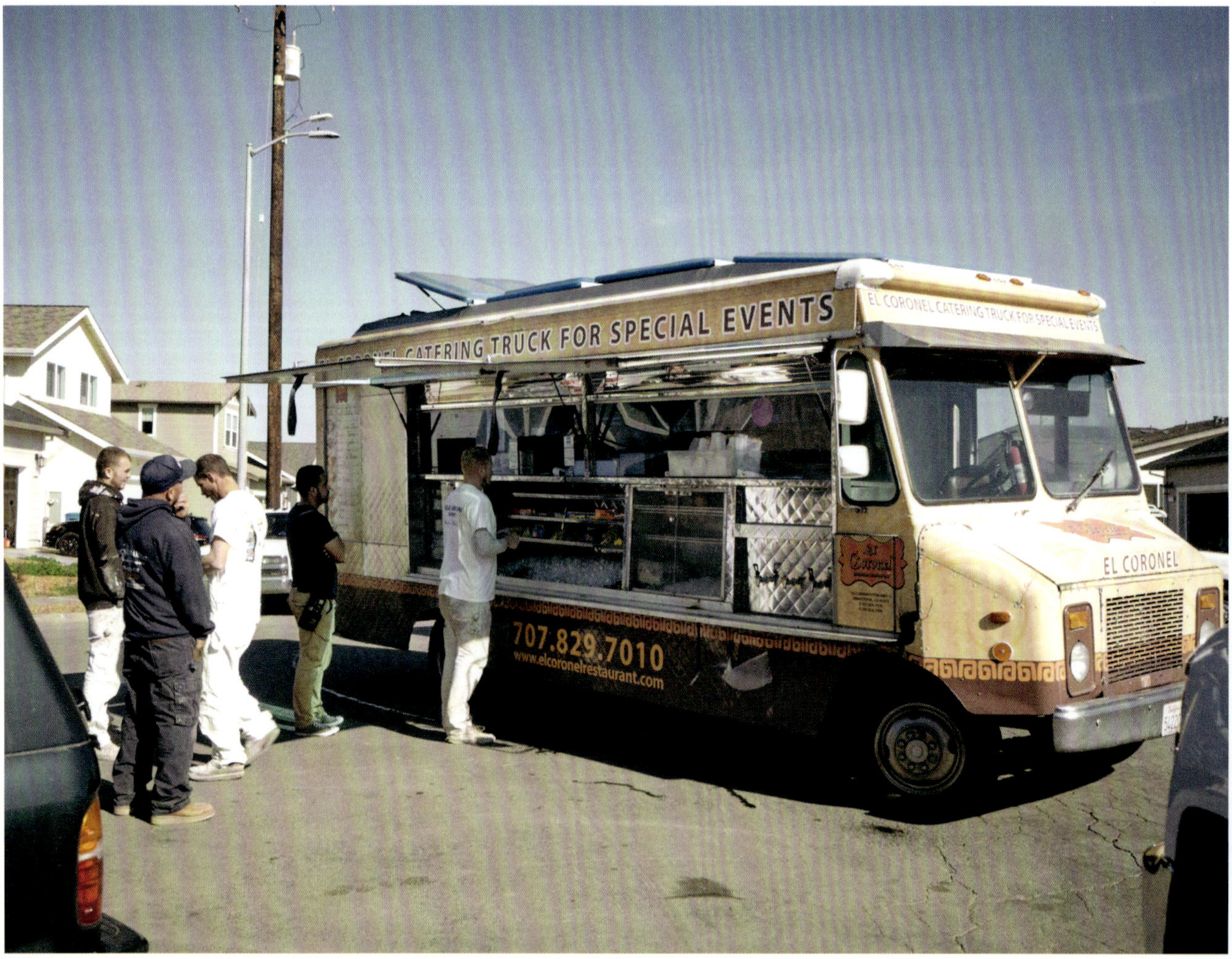
CATERING TRUCK FOR SPECIAL EVENTS
EL CORONEL CATERING TRUCK FOR SPECIAL EVENTS
El Coronel
EL CORONEL
707.829.7010
www.elcoronelrestaurant.com

American Framing
Pavilion of the United States at the
17th International Architecture Exhibition –
La Biennale di Venezia

Co-curators
Paul Andersen and Paul Preissner

Benches
Ania Jaworska

Furniture
Norman Kelley

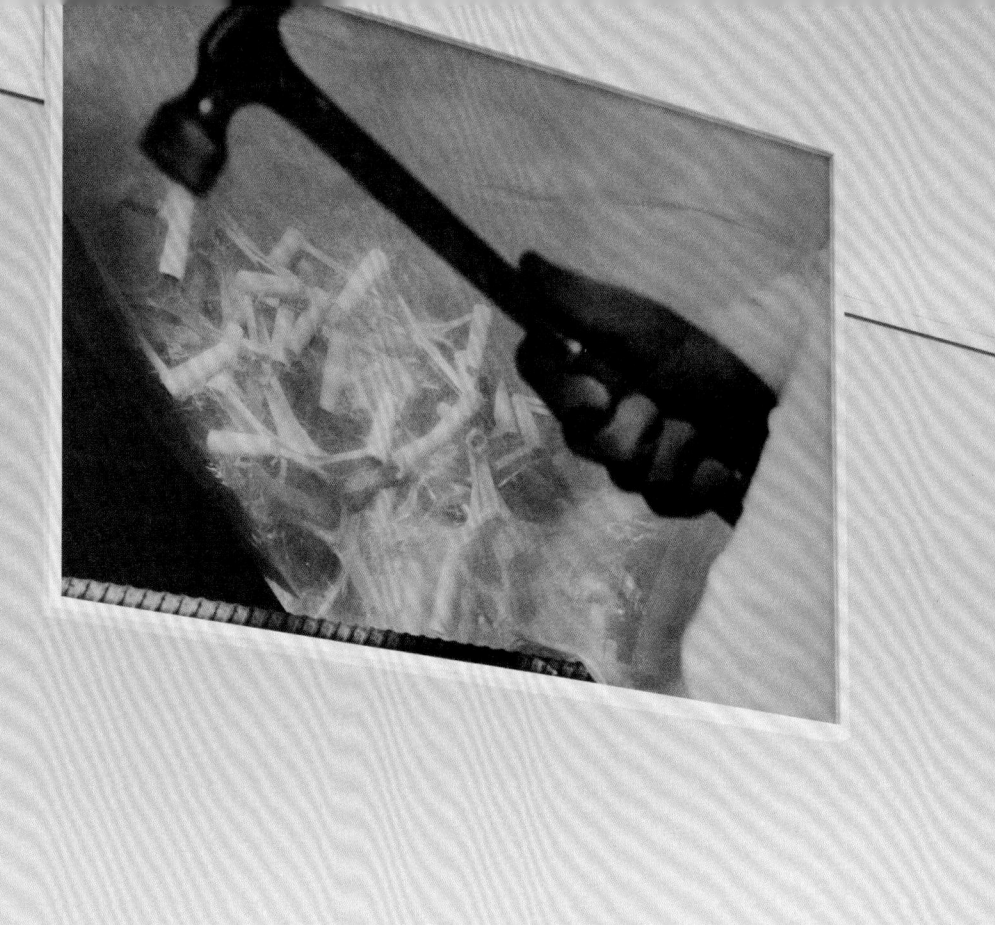

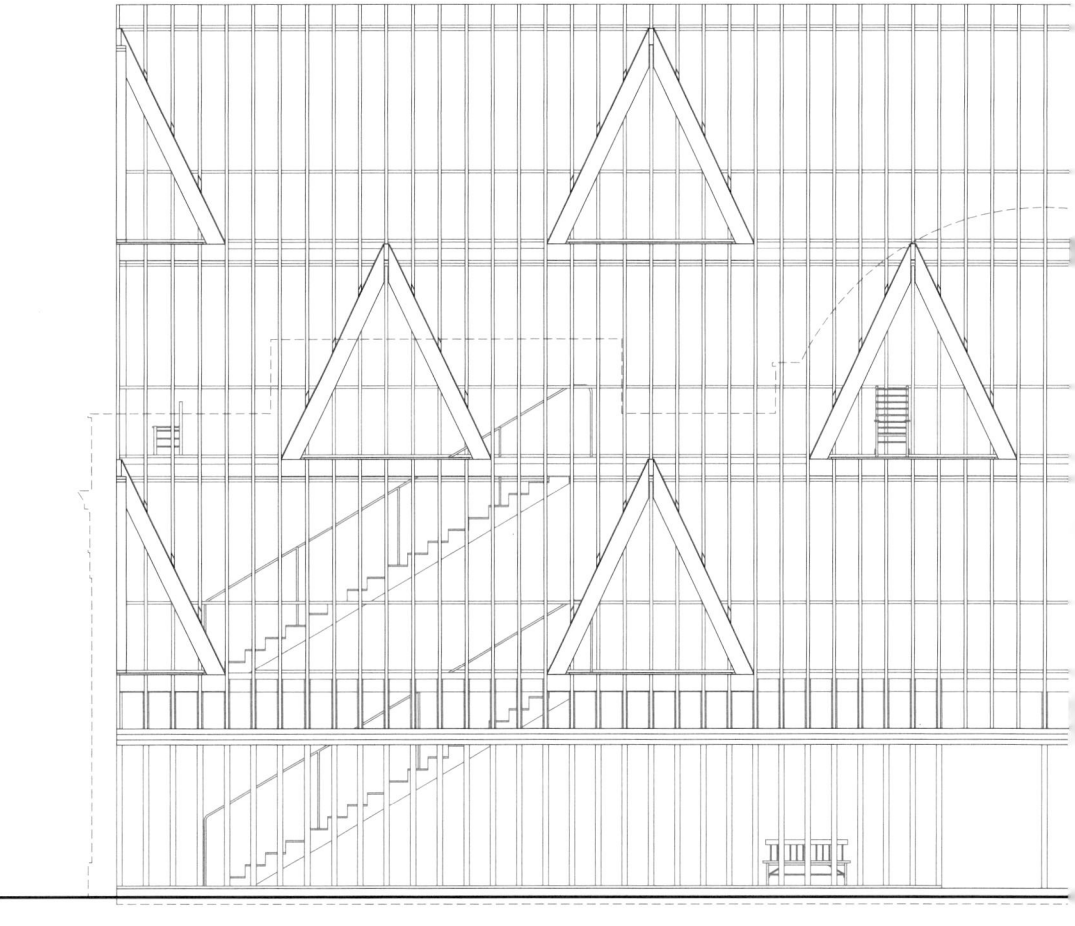

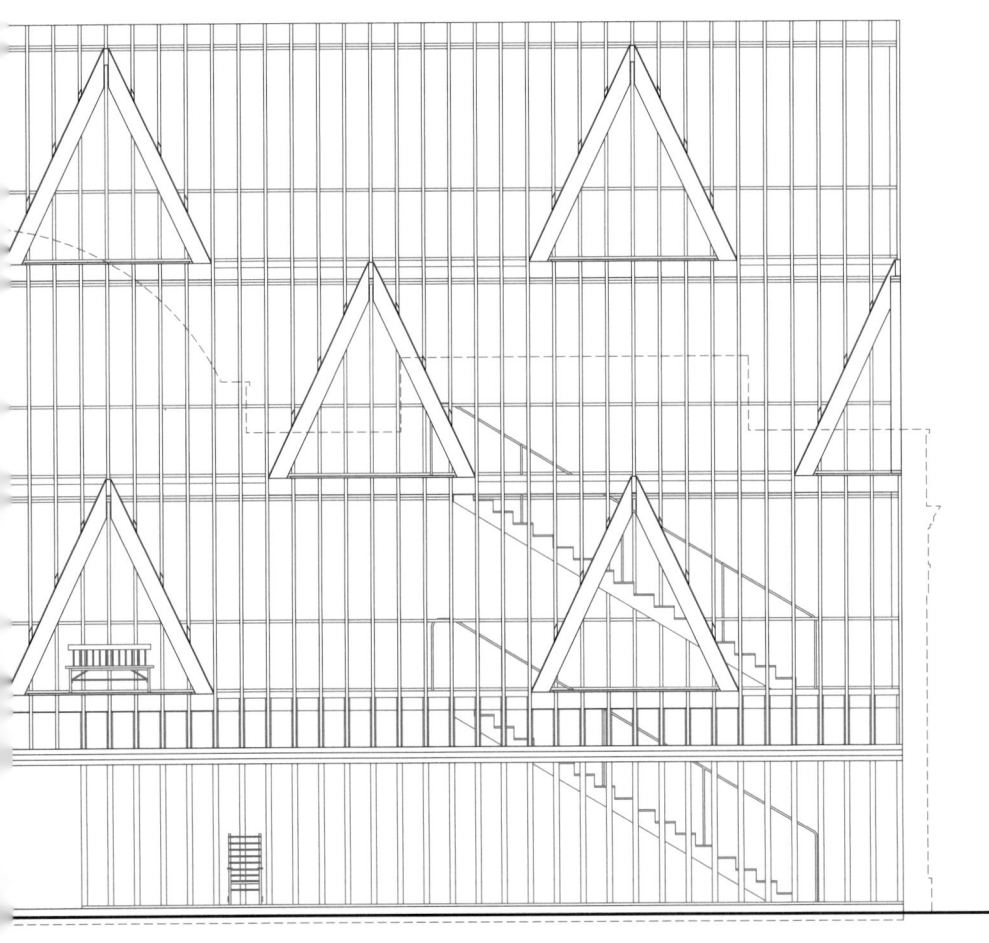

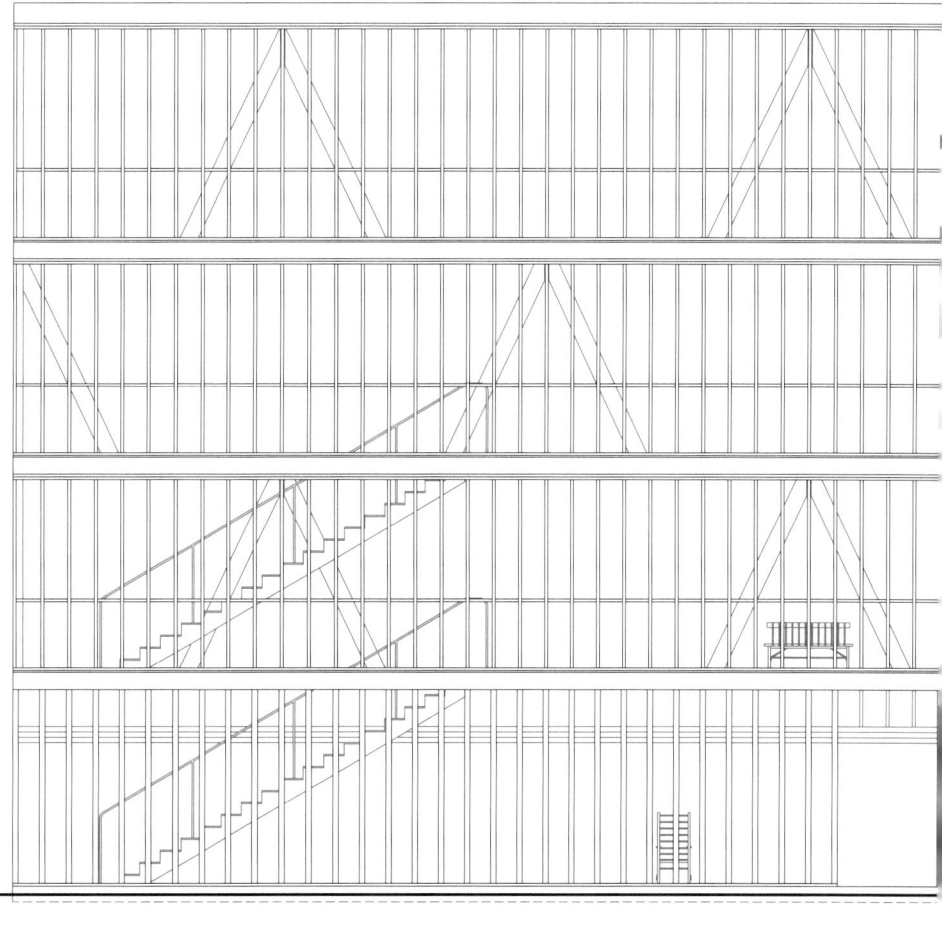

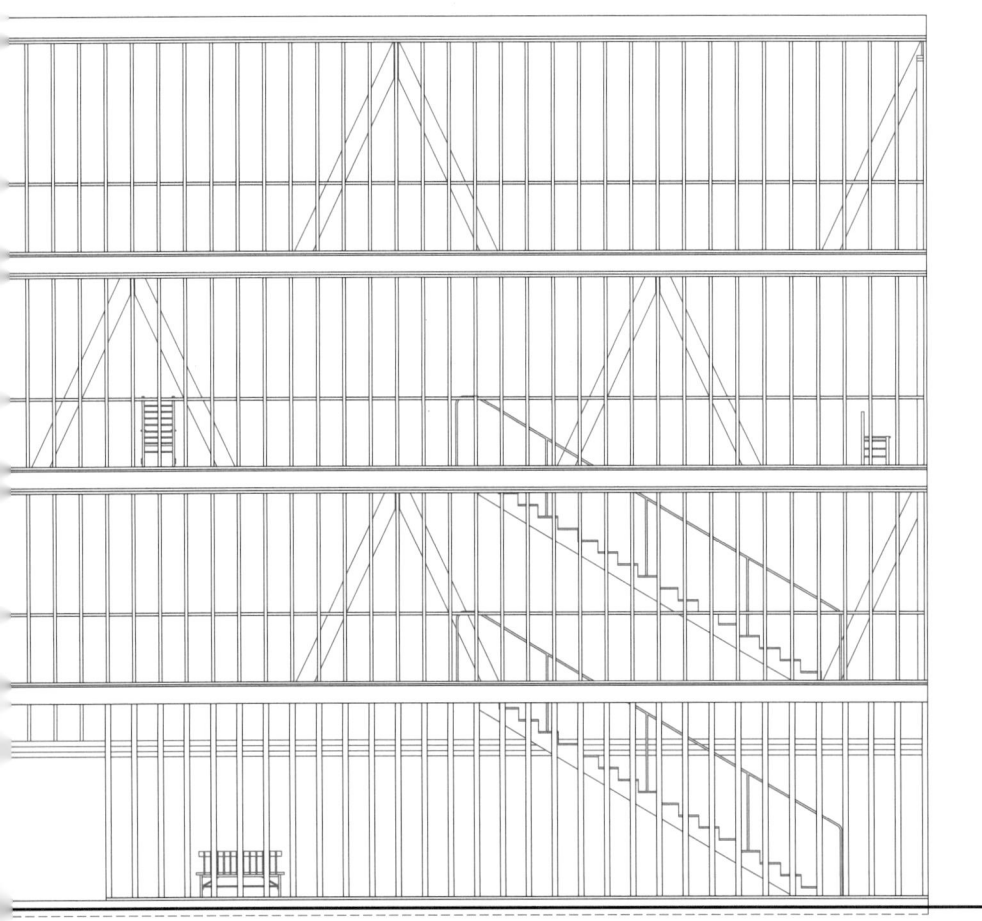

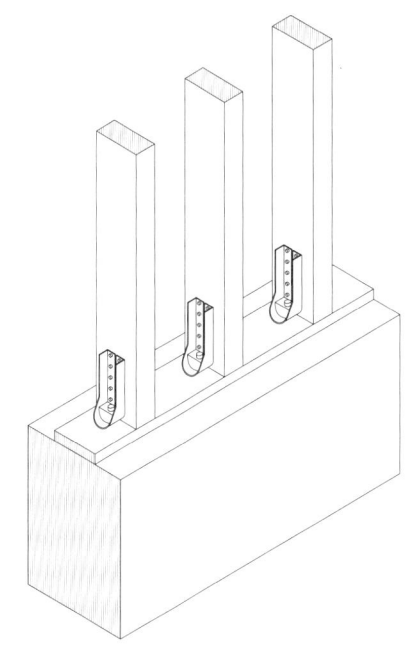

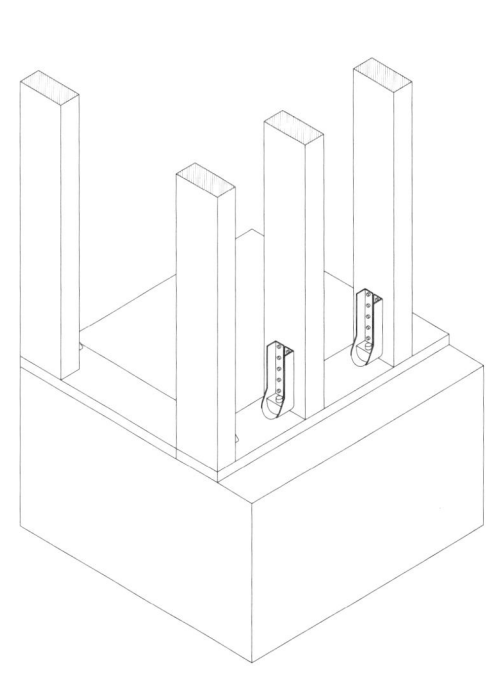

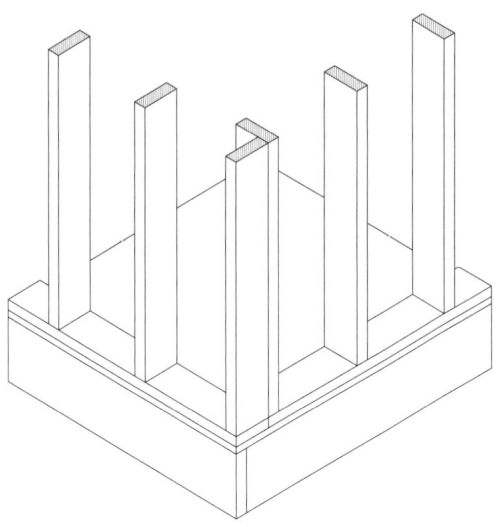
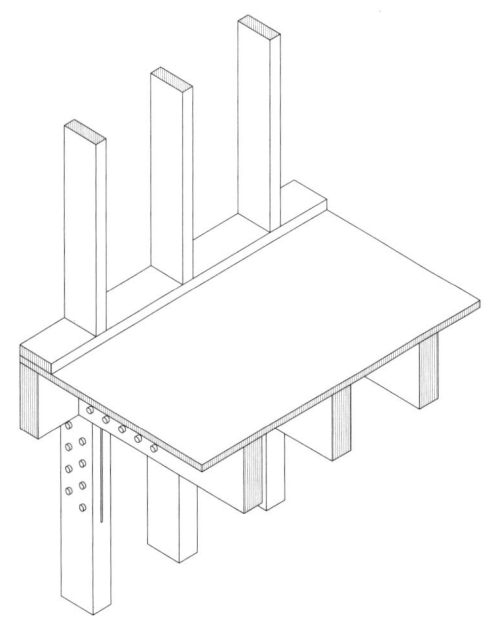

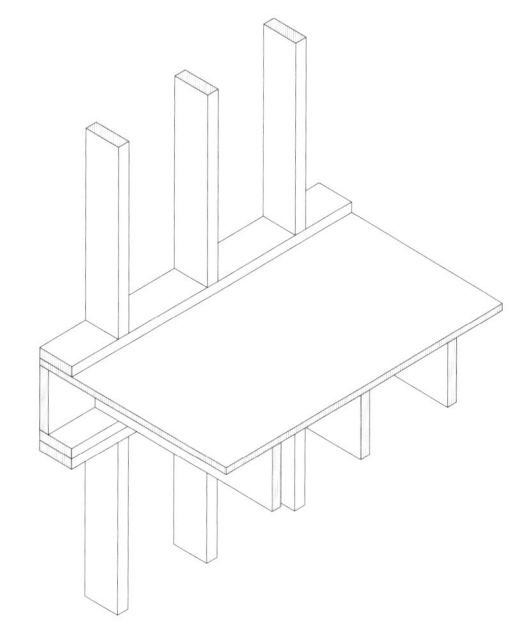
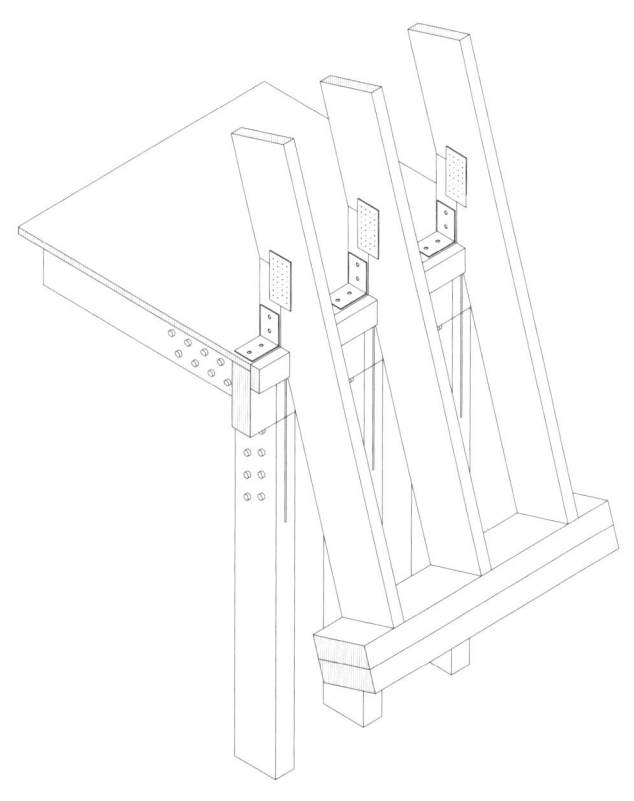

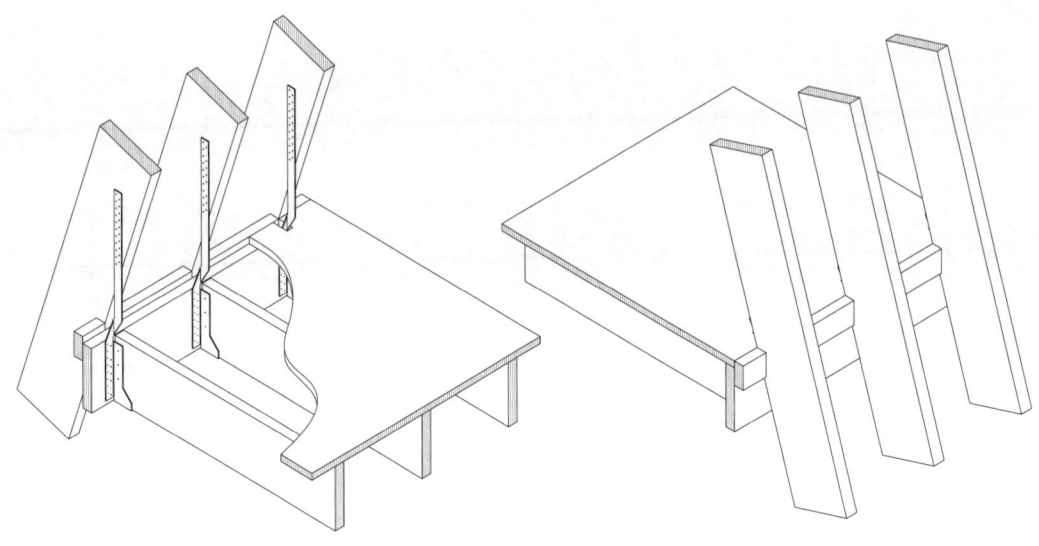
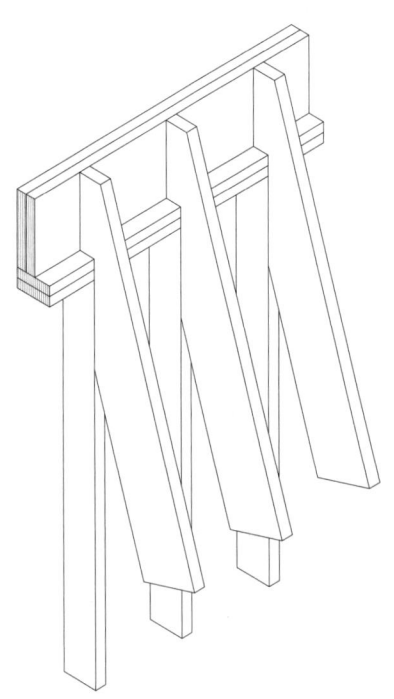

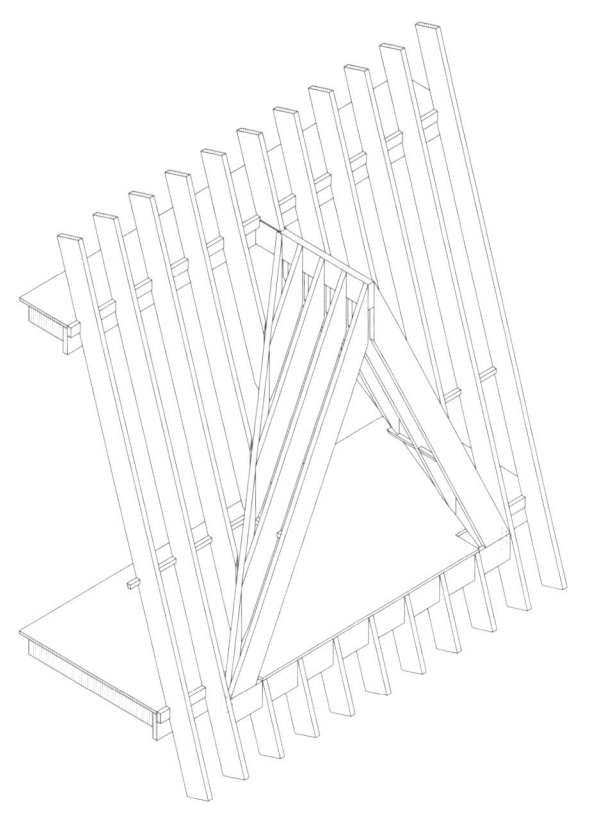

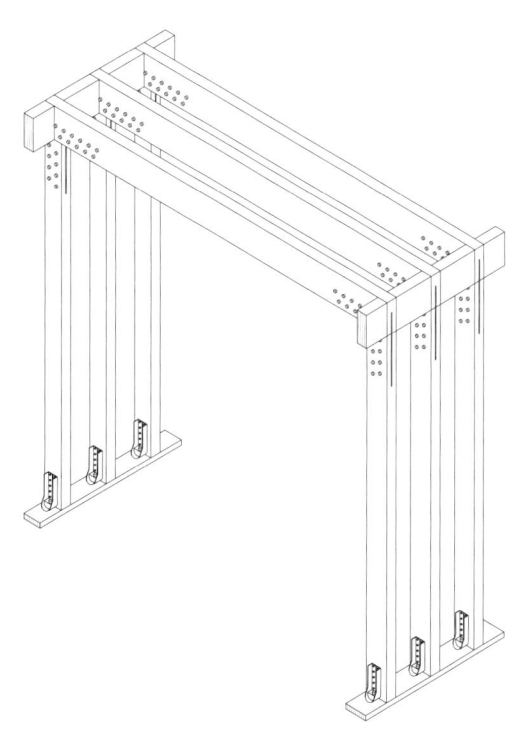

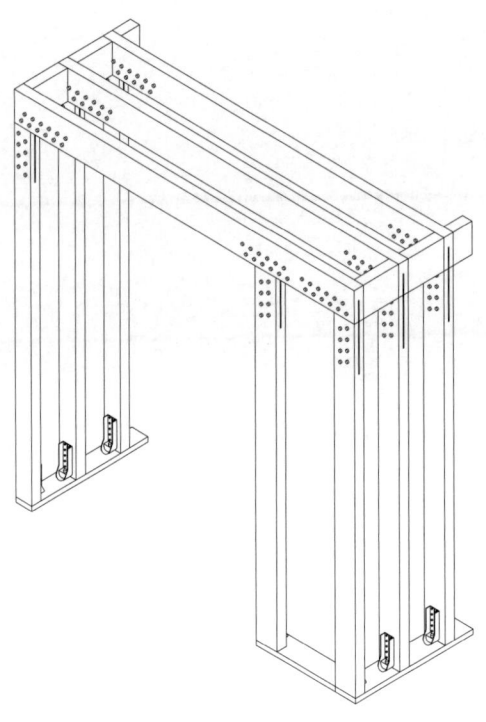
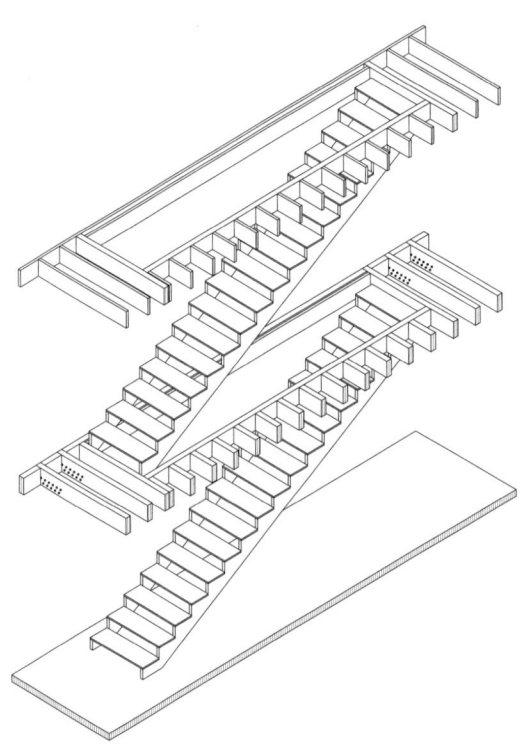

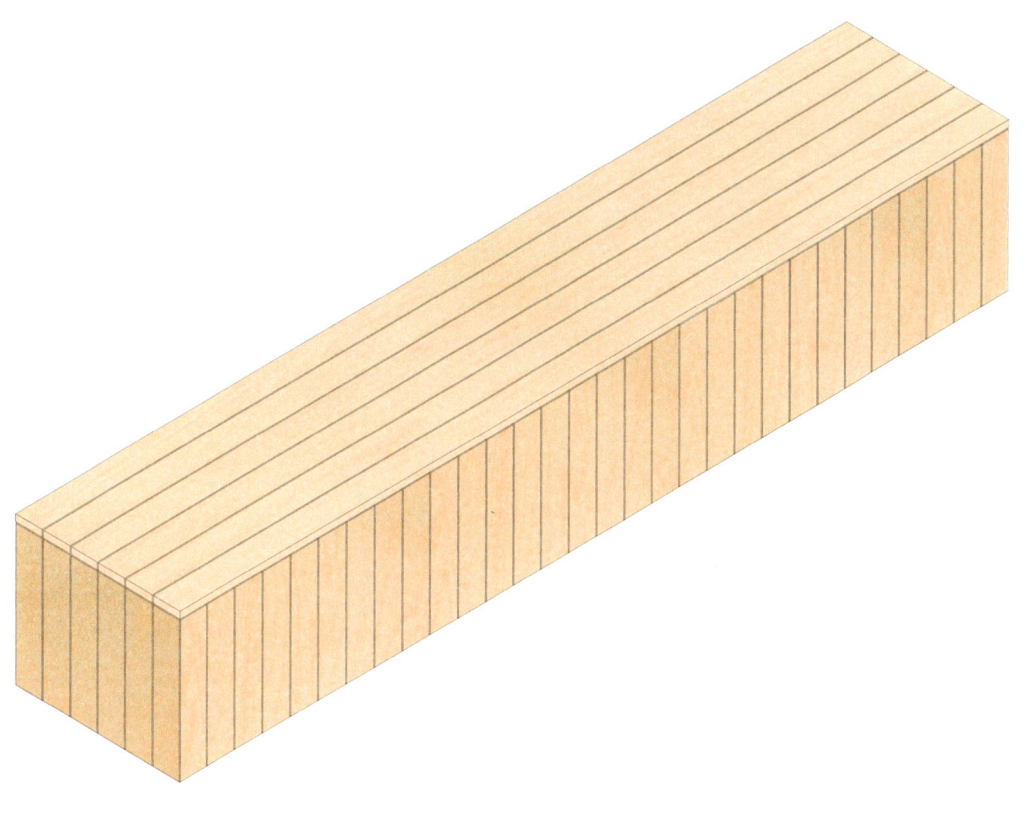

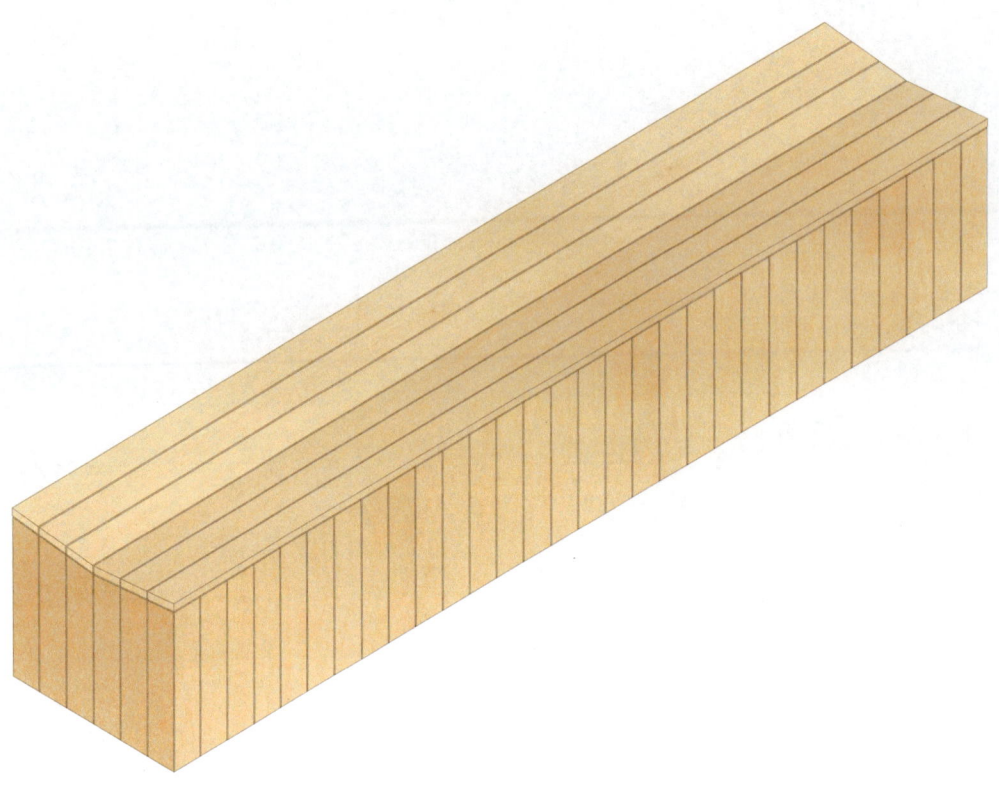
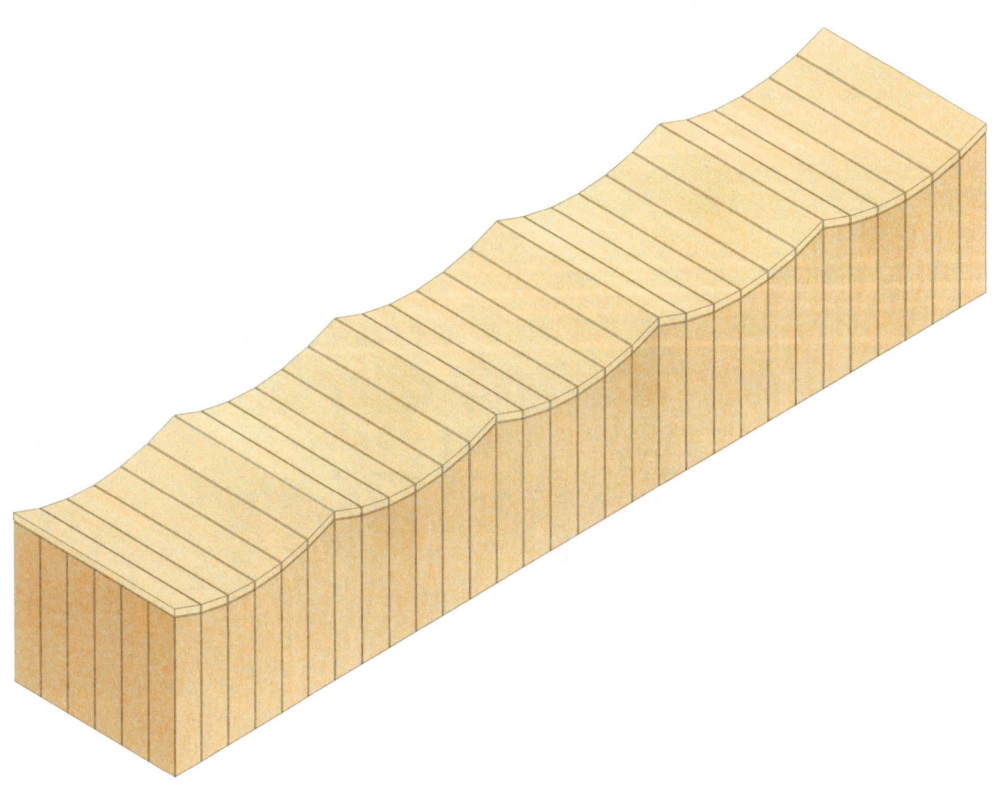

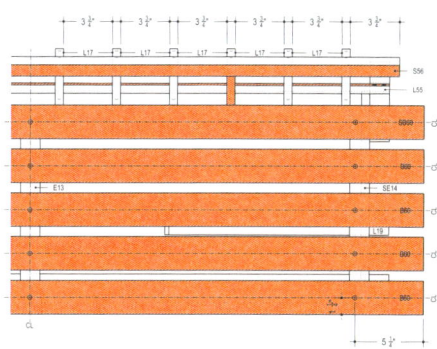
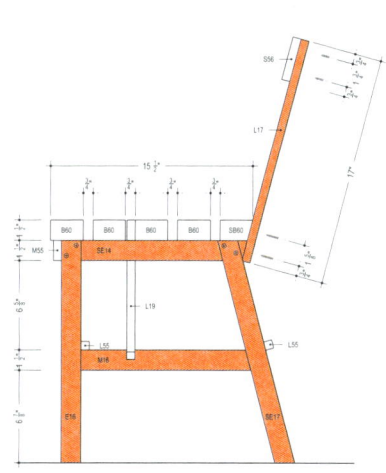
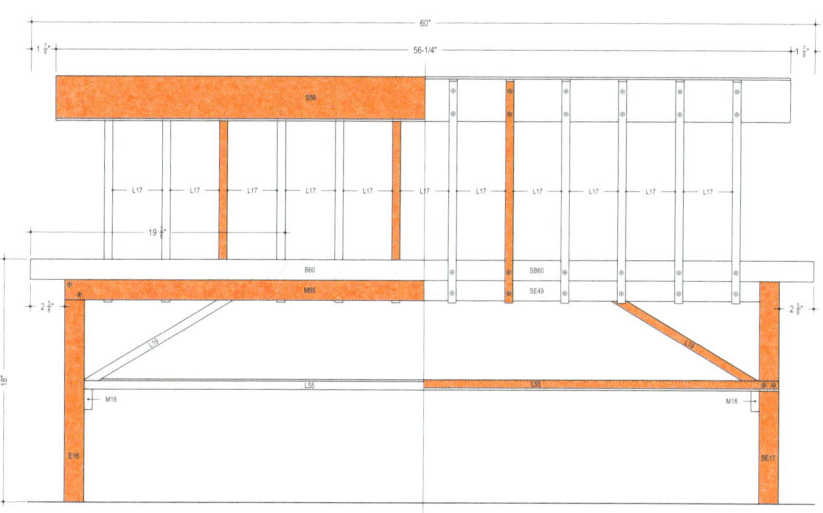

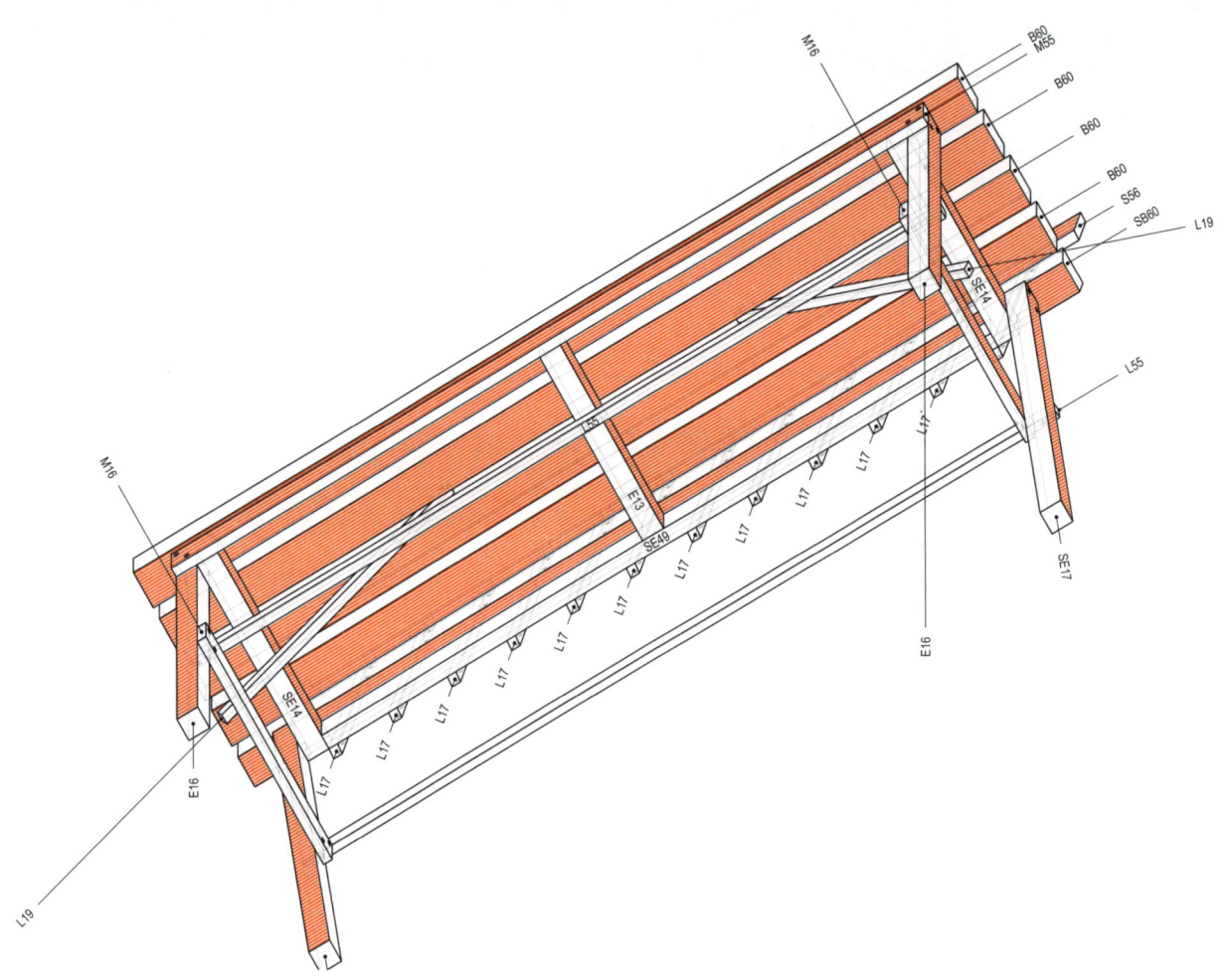

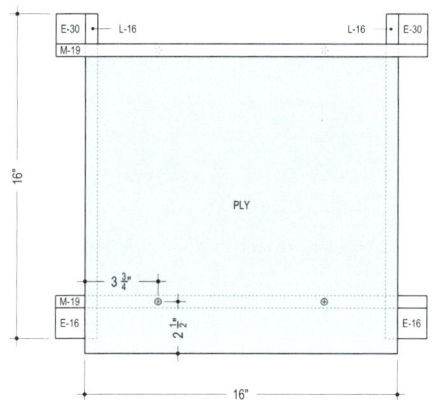
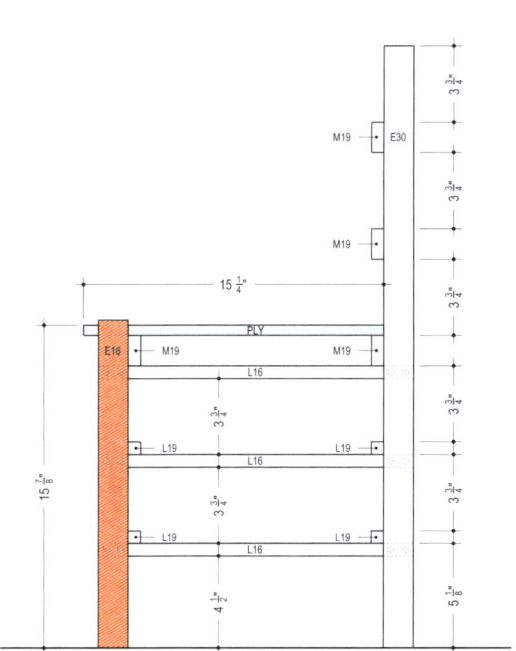
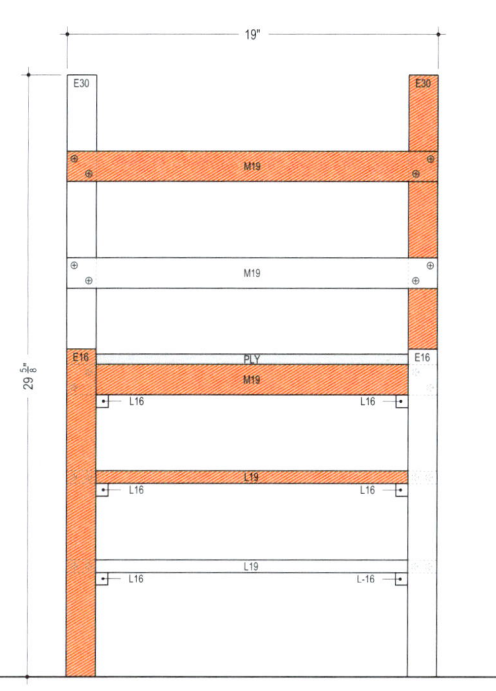

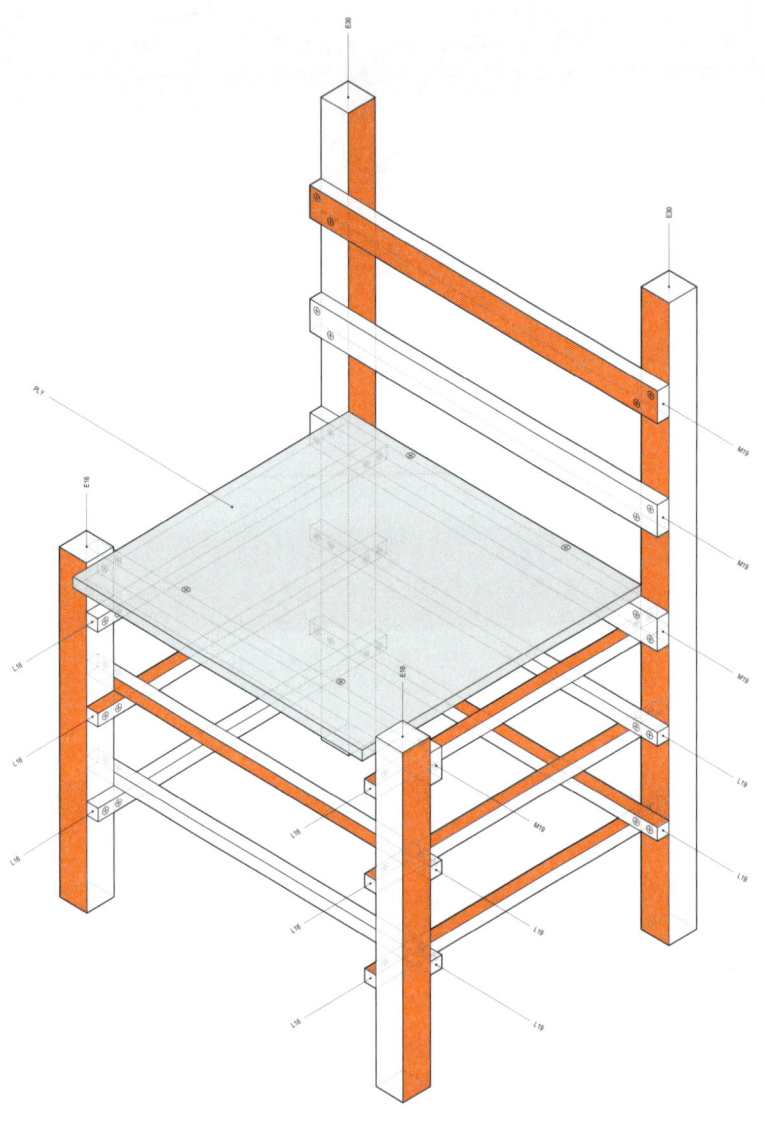

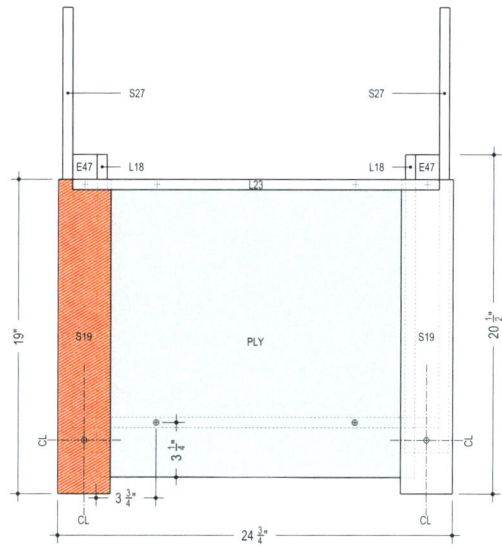
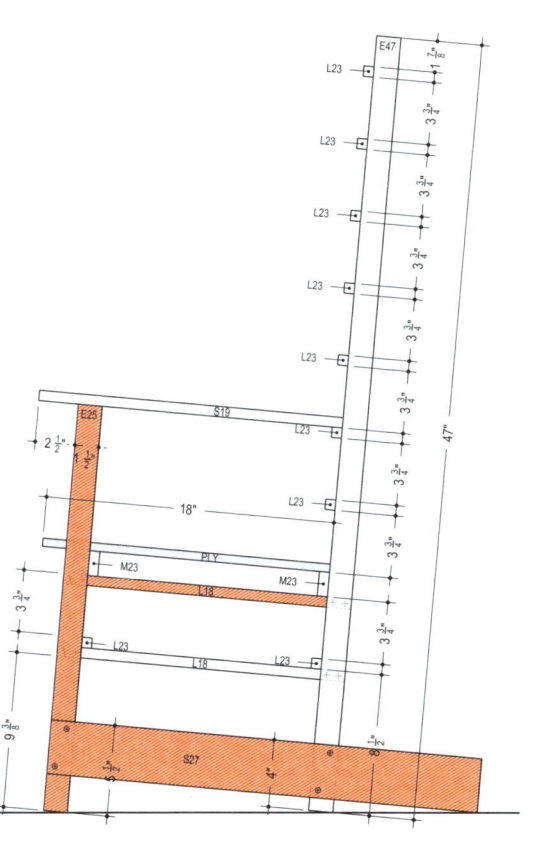
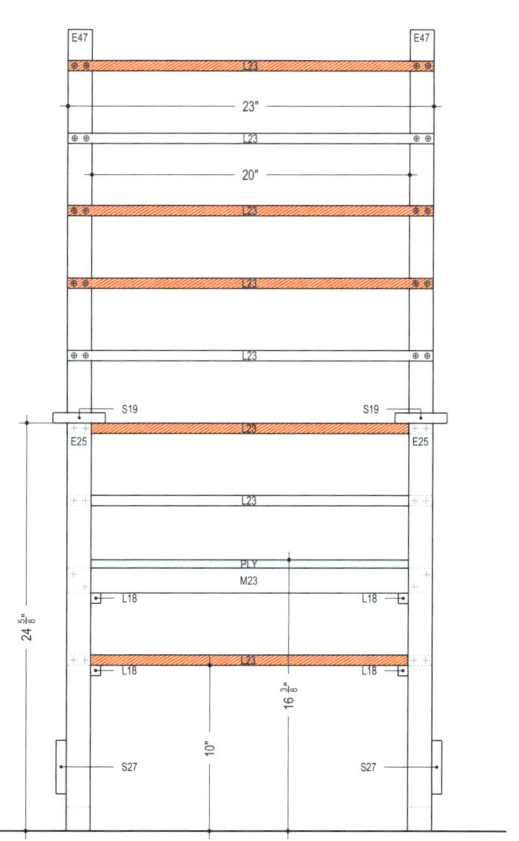

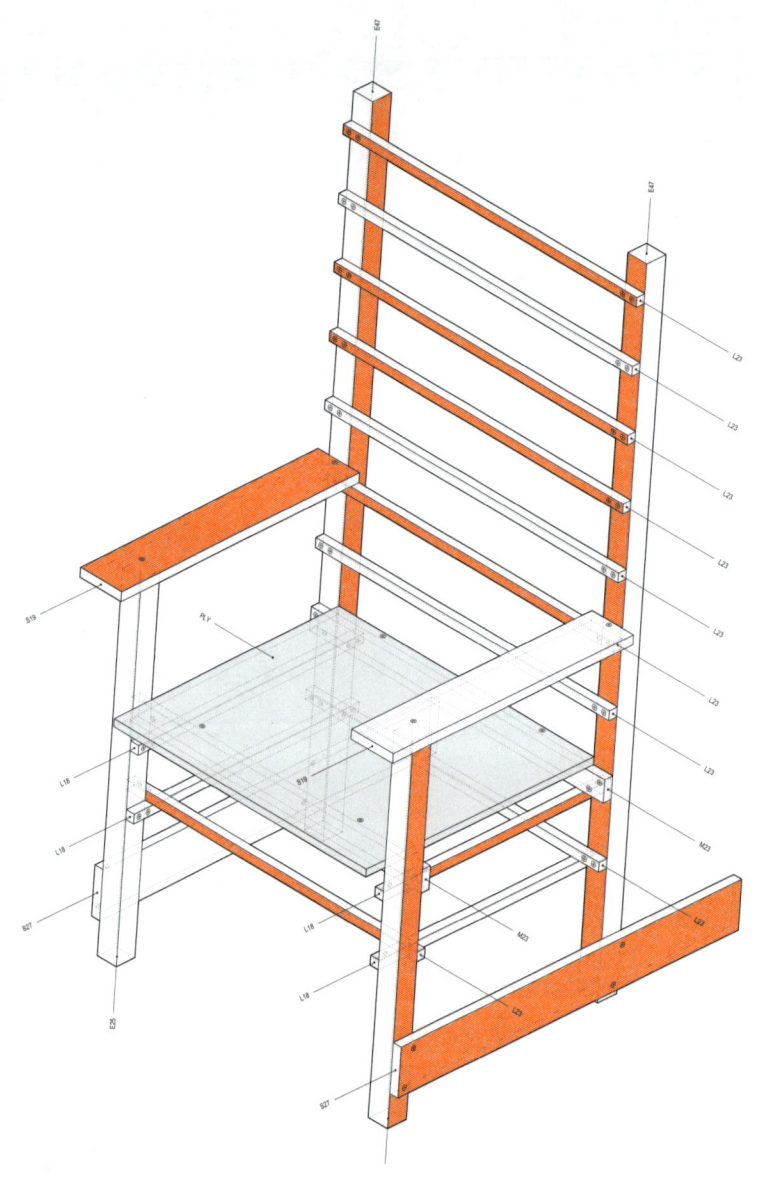

Examples from history

Warehouse
George Washington Snow
Chicago, 1832

Softwood framing developed incrementally over many years and in many places across the Midwest, so it is impossible to credit its origin to any one person or building. Snow's warehouse is the earliest individual building that historians have identified. Despite its significance, no photos or drawings of it survive. Did it really exist or is it a historian's myth? What did it look like? The size and geometry of its site at the mouth of the Chicago River, combined with descriptions of similar warehouses in the area and construction methods of the time, provide enough clues to reconstruct Snow's building.

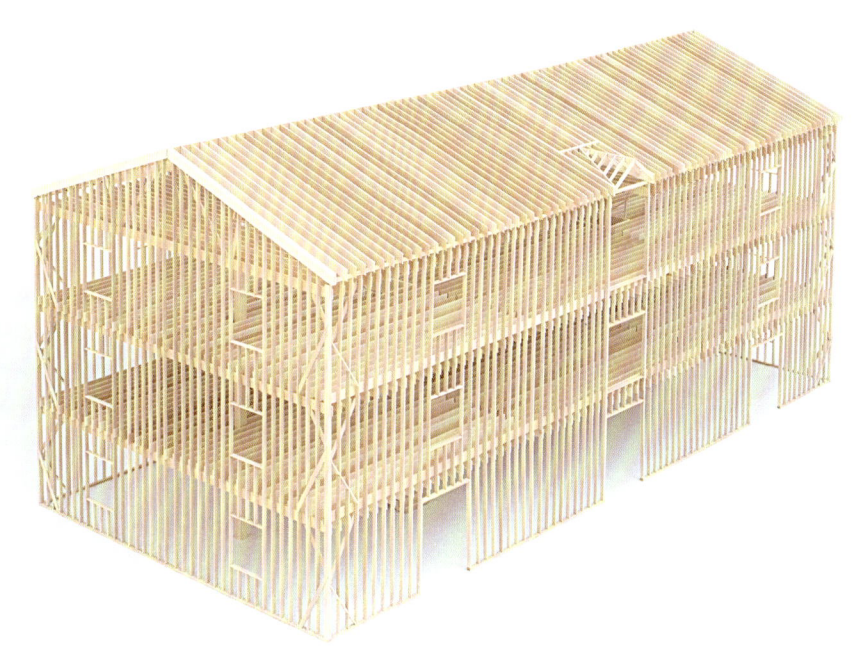

"A Cheap Farm-House"
Solon Robinson
American Agriculturist, February 1846

Robinson, a farmer and entrepreneur living in Indiana, was an early proponent of lightweight framing. He frequently wrote articles extolling its affordability, adaptability, and ease of use. Beginning in the late 1840s, he supplemented his written descriptions with drawings, including plans for this cheap farmhouse. To make the house more affordable, it was designed to be built in stages.

Blockhouse
American prairie, late 1800s

The blockhouse was a short-lived building type constructed in frontier forts during the American Indian Wars. Blockhouses had small windows to limit their inhabitants' vulnerability to enemy fire. The windows' size also made it hard to see out, so the upper floor was rotated 45 degrees. Soldiers positioned on the two levels were able to scan the surrounding territory better with windows facing eight directions rather than four. A redundant assembly of 2×4s in the walls of the lower level enabled the building to take such an odd form. The angle of the upper floor could be established in response to site conditions, with little effect on structural performance. Just a few decades after it first appeared, the blockhouse was obsolete. Settler colonial violence and disease had decimated the population of Indigenous Americans.

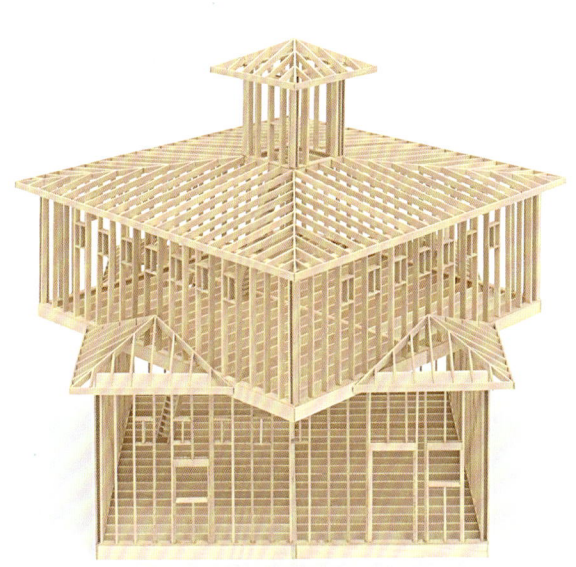

Lumber

The American lumber industry, which consumes approximately 18 percent of the timber cut in North America each year, began with colonial timber speculation. Having used up their own old-growth forests and needing wood for shipbuilding, fuel for their iron industry, and firewood, the British sought out forests in the New World. Timber was a valuable resource for settlers, who increasingly relied on wood for building construction. Prior to the mid-1800s, most wood was cut and used locally, leading to a variety of approaches to sizing. As the lumber industry consolidated, so did the need for standardized dimensions and quality. The first national standards were established by the Central Committee on Lumber Standards in 1924 and have been revised several times.

The notational dimensions of a piece of lumber have always been larger than a board's actual size. Early on, nominal dimensions referred to the green, rough cut. Once dried and planed smooth, the finished board was smaller. In the late nineteenth century, a 2×4 that had been planed on all four sides (most were planed on only one or two sides) was 1¾ inches by 3¾ inches. The size was reduced as the industry discovered that lighter framing is more economical and still structurally stable. Since 1964, a standard 2×4 measures 1½ inches by 3½ inches.

Earthquake cottages
San Francisco, 1906

On the morning of April 18, 1906, an earthquake destroyed more than five hundred city blocks of San Francisco and left more than half of the city's 400,000 residents without housing. In response, the newly formed San Francisco Relief Corporation, the San Francisco Parks Commission, the United States Army, and union carpenters cooperatively built 5,610 cottages in eleven camps around the city. Most were either 10 feet by 14 feet or 14 feet by 18 feet. Tenants paid $2 per month until the $50 cottages were paid off—a price that allowed many residents to own a home for the first time. Once they'd paid off their cottages, owners were required to move the structures from the camps to inexpensive lots made available around the city, typically on horse-drawn carts or skids. A handful of the 5,343 relocated cottages still stand today.

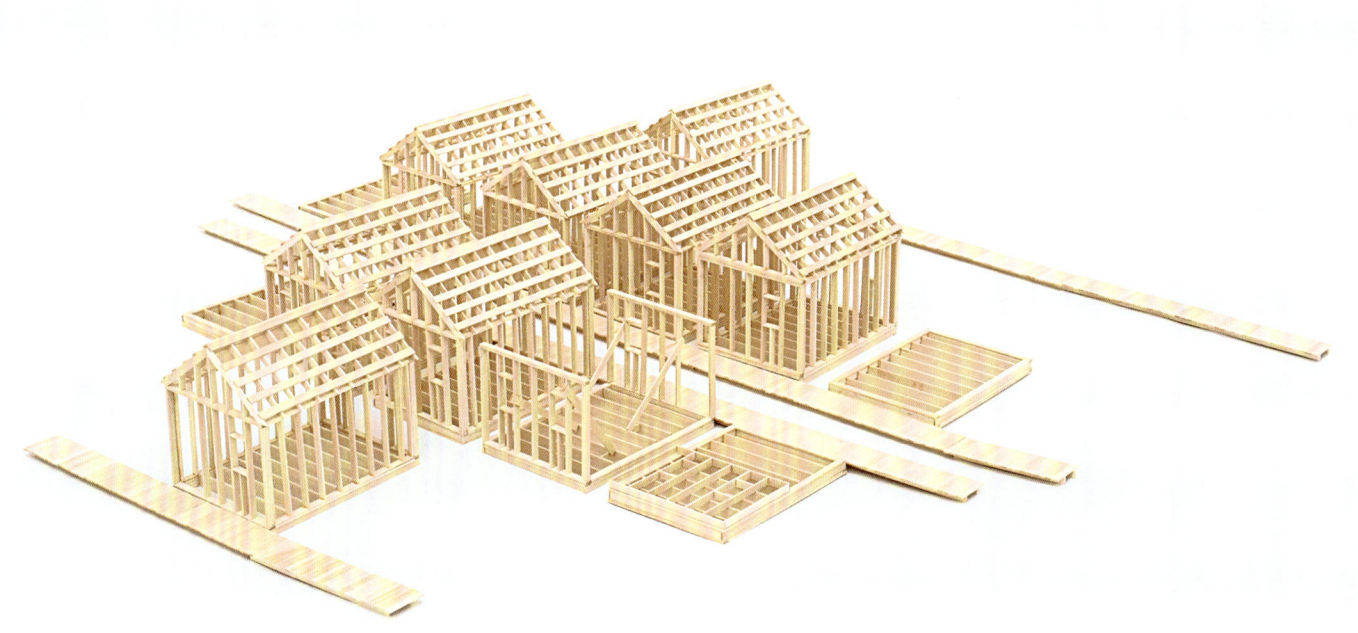

The Hillsboro (no. 3308)
Sears Modern Homes catalog, 1930–37

Over 100,000 houses were sold through Sears's modern homes program between 1908 and 1940. All the materials needed to build a given model were delivered to the building site, from precut lumber and carved wood staircases to nails and varnish. Mass production lowered labor costs by an estimated 40 percent, while an extensive array of sizes, forms, and styles ensured variety within neighborhoods. The Sears homes collectively anticipated both the broad spectrum of wood-frame house designs that evolved in the mid-twentieth century and the economic ground rules that limited architectural experimentation.

Pallet
George G. Raymond
US patent no. 2178646, 1937

Pallets were patented as early as the 1920s and began to be used extensively to move materials during the Second World War. Standard stringer pallets, the most common type, measure 48 inches by 48 inches and can be lifted from two sides by a jack or forklift. The cheapest pallets are made of softwood and are often considered expendable. They consume 15 percent of US-produced softwood lumber.

Spike's doghouse
Tom and Jerry, 1952

A fundamental and identifiable feature of the American landscape, wood framing frequently shows up in cartoons, comic strips, and movies, often as part of a banal backdrop against which farfetched events play out. In one episode of *Tom and Jerry*, the cat and mouse's neighbor Spike makes plans to build himself a new doghouse. Regrettably, every time Tom chases Jerry through the scene, he destroys Spike's partially constructed house in a different way.

A-frame
Henrik Bull
Stowe, Vermont, 1953

Many cultures have their own version of the A-frame, with expressions as varied as Polynesian pole houses and Wienerschnitzel drive-thrus. Henrik Bull and his classmate John Flender built this house in a single summer, between semesters of architecture school. Though most wood-framed houses take irregular forms, this one is a perfect triangular prism. All of its edges are 26 feet, its section is an equilateral triangle, and the floor and both roof planes are square.

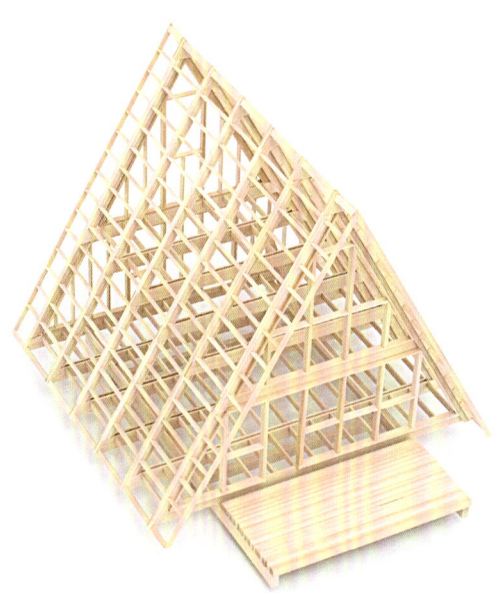

The Vista-Liner
Smoker Lumber Company
New Paris, Indiana, 1956

A lightweight wood frame is ideal for mobile homes, descendants of the covered wagon that are built in a factory on a permanent chassis and then moved to a site. (Pallets are also a common skirting material for the homes.) This type of housing was especially popular in the 1950s and 1960s, the heyday of Harley Earl and GM's Art and Color Section. Similar to how car manufacturers released new models every year, the styling of mobile homes evolved continually.

Prior to 1956, mobile homes were 8 feet wide, the maximum width that the Department of Transportation allowed to be towed behind a car. When manufacturers began delivering homes with commercial trucks, the maximum width expanded to 10 feet, a feature that distinguished mobile homes from RVs and trailers. Models like the Vista-Liner offered many of the luxuries of a typical suburban home in a more affordable package. The Vista-Liner's tri-level layout included a kitchen, living room, two bathrooms, and four bedrooms stacked at the rear.

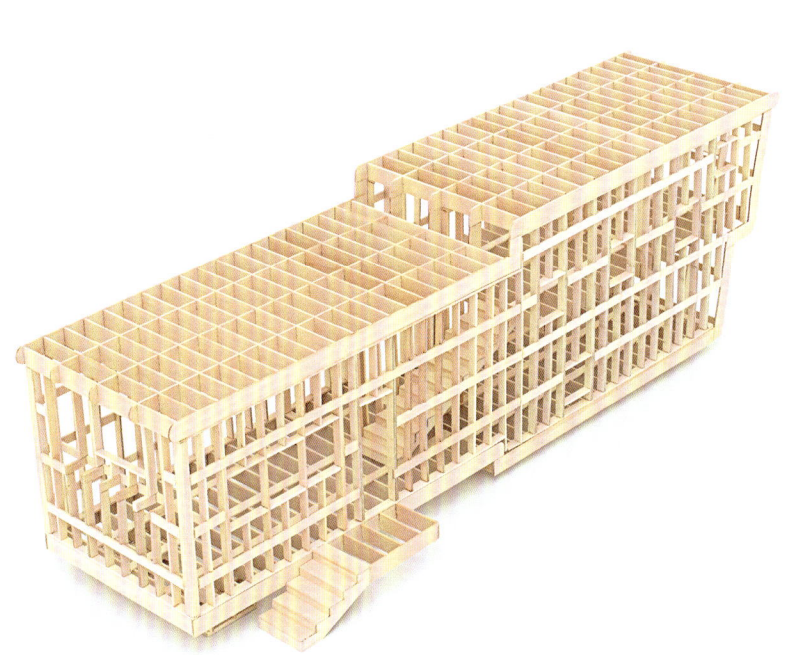

Cartop Dome
Trinidad, Colorado, 1966

The founders of Drop City, a countercultural artists' community established in 1965, built eight geodesic domes with amateur knowledge of Buckminster Fuller's research, almost no construction experience, and mostly salvaged materials. They determined the impromptu geometry of each dome as it was built, according to its particular needs. Cartop Dome, a wonky polyhedral house, was made of reused lumber, doors, and windows and covered with chopped-out car tops.

Photographs
Daniel Shea

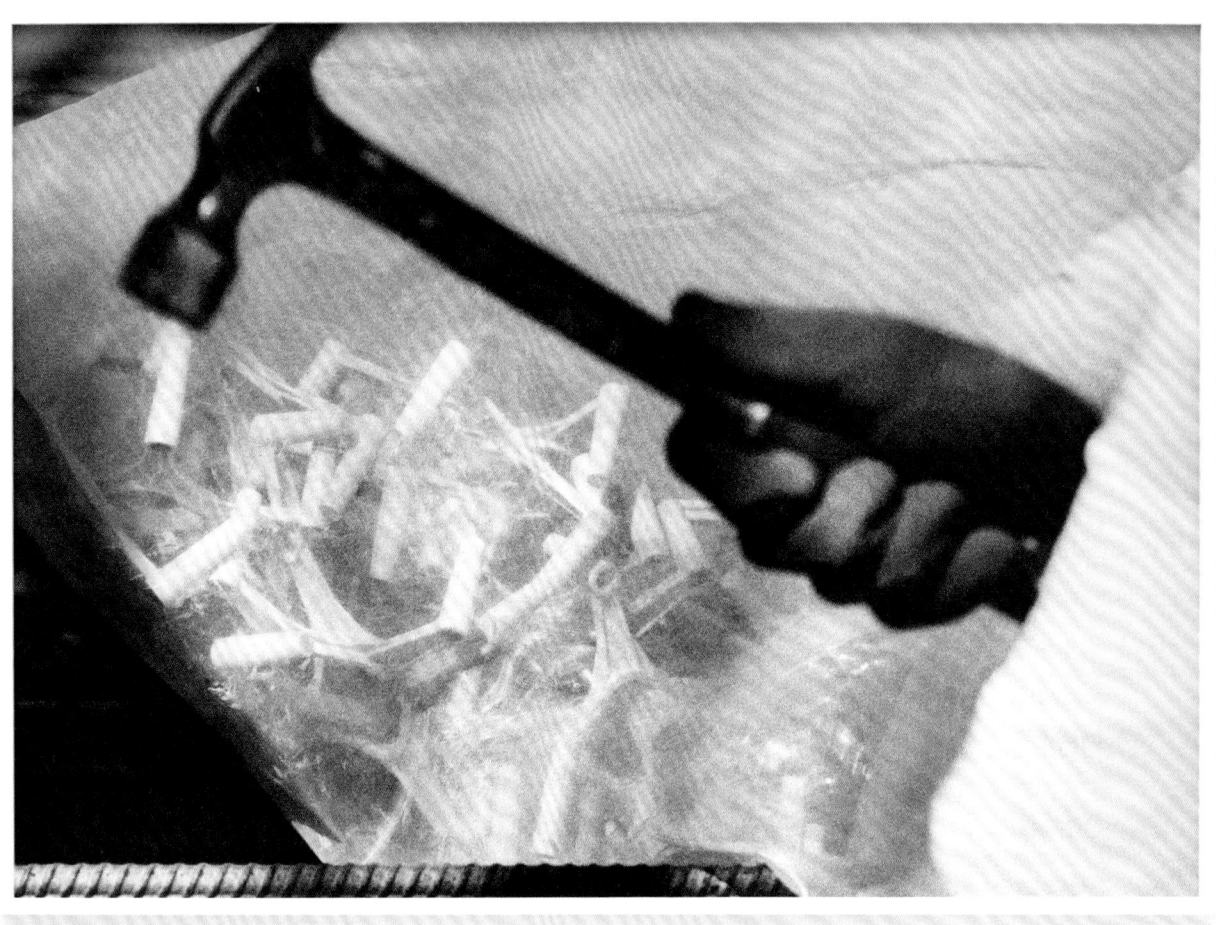

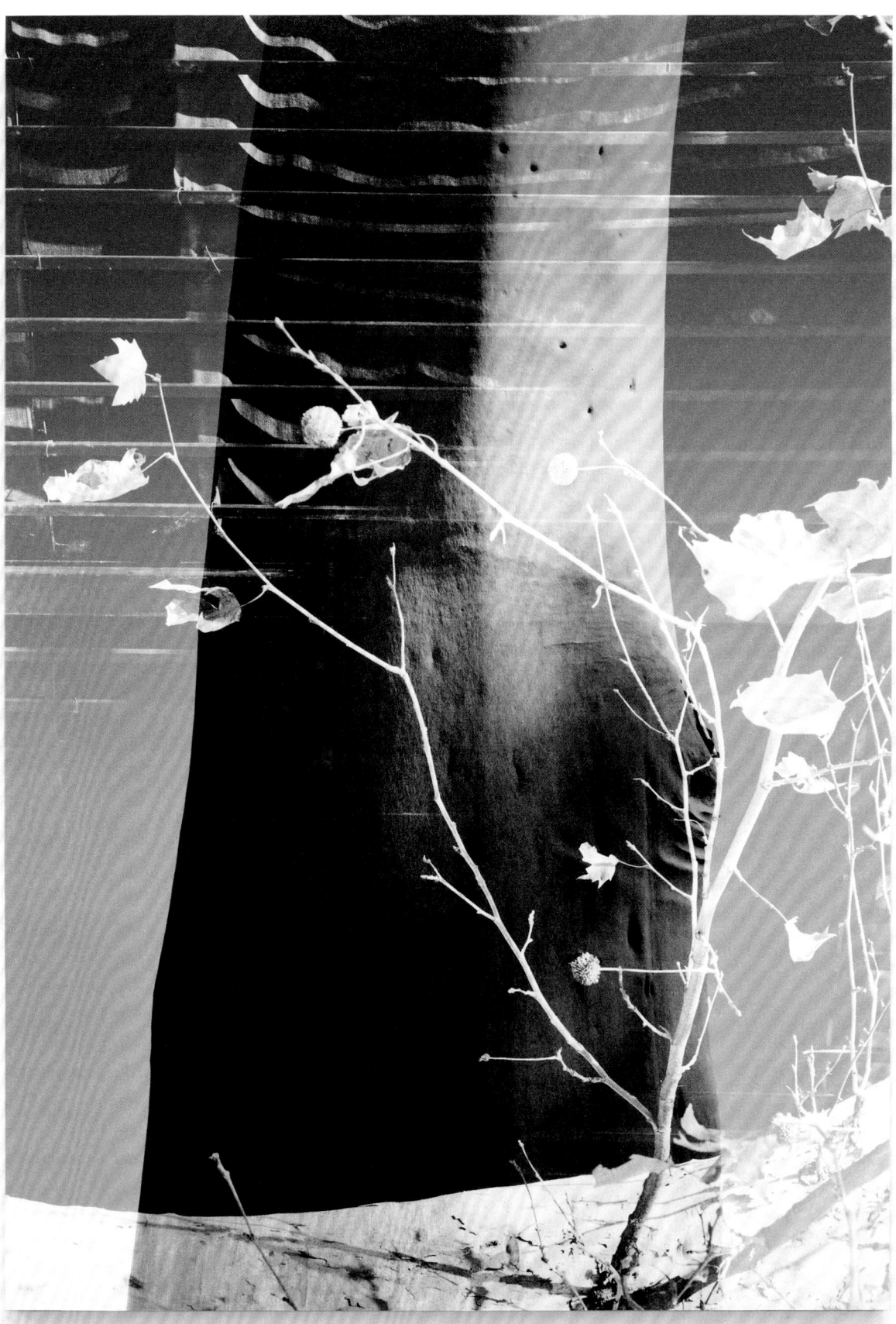

Architecture *Americana*
Penelope Dean

Interest in the wood frame is nothing new. Some might even say it's as old as Adam. But in recent years it has regained currency as historians and designers broadly reorient their discourse and research away from front-stage acts (aesthetics, iconicity, authorship) to behind-the-scenes conditions (social practices, labor relations, construction procedures, business collaborations, corporate logistics) in an effort to change entrenched habits and biases of architectural practice and history, while laying claim to new research niches. The wood frame has historically and conveniently served both concerns because it is characterized by a distinctive lack of ownership: anyone—contractor, critic, designer, developer, DIY-er, historian, theorist—can use it, deploy it as a medium of innovation, an emblem of mass production, an instrument of specification, an icon of sustainability, or a building technology. As one of the principal claims of Paul Andersen and Paul Preissner's *American Framing*, the discursive positioning of the frame as a symbol of social equivalence among citizen-consumers—"the same something for everyone"—represents a conspicuous urgency to assert what Colin Rowe once identified as architecture's *morale-word* (collective social concern) over its *physique-flesh* (form).[1] Or to put it another way, the dimension the frame occupies is, as Jean Baudrillard put it in another context, "captive to the moral dimension which it is [its] job to signify."[2]

The temporary, freestanding wooden structure that Andersen and Preissner built in front of the existing neoclassical US Pavilion in Venice, designed by William Adams Delano and Chester Holmes Aldrich in 1930, appears to contradict this contemporary trend. At 1:1 scale, with a pitched roof straight from the American dream, the wood frame has been staged in what at first glance appears to be an unsurprising manner, recognizably domestic, quintessentially vernacular. It emphasizes the physique that Rowe identified in experimental domestic architecture during the 1960s and 1970s, but without any of the theoretical explication. Here, architecture follows the example of well-behaved children: it is seen but not heard. This discursive silence is attributable to the exigency the architects feel obligated to address, as well as to their divergent architectural ambitions: while Andersen seeks to elevate the vernacular into architecture, Preissner aims to deflate architecture into something else. The collision of these two American narratives—"rags to riches" meets "more for less"—finds expression in wood-frame construction precisely because the frame is materially, and conceptually, ductile.

The architectural effects of this shotgun marriage of oppositions are striking. While there might not be anything surprising about yet another structure built with 2×4s (although technically, they are only nominally), and nothing new in terms of subject matter, and hardly

---

1   Colin Rowe, "Introduction," in *Five Architects* (New York: Oxford University Press, 1975), 7. If Rowe defined modern architecture's morale along European lines of "socialist mission" ("a vision of a new and better world"), Andersen and Preissner identify morale as already realized in market capitalism—i.e., the ubiquity of wood-frame construction as evidence of social equity. The framing also recalls Le Corbusier's characterization of whitewash: "the wealth of the poor and of the rich—of everybody, just as bread, milk and water are the wealth of the slave and of the king." Le Corbusier, "A Coat of Whitewash: The Law of Ripolin," in *The Decorative Art of Today*, trans. James I. Dunnett (London: Architectural Press, 1987), 192.
2   Jean Baudrillard, "Structures of Interior Design," *The System of Objects*, trans. James Benedict (London: Verso, 1996), 16. Originally published in 1968.

anything unique in terms of posing or expressing the problem, the collision of it all, and the impeccable diligence with which the new structure has been designed, advances an architecture of such generality that it is possible to comprehend the design in highly differentiated ways, and often in ways completely at odds with one another. The structure channels people, precedents, history, and furniture in ways that exceed materiality, design methods, and even the architects' own rhetoric. In other words, from generality, ambiguities and contradictions sprout. Notably, this generality does not emerge through a curatorial operation, but through the explicit act of architectural design.

First, there is the dramatic effacing quality of the "addition" as a typological and technological construct. Inserted just in front of—rather than behind—the pavilion, on a concrete plinth, the frame affords a new entry. From the front, the bulk of the elevation reads as a McMansion-esque roof punctuated by overscaled and flattened dormers—a decisive domestic facade to the Giardini forecourt. From behind, a gigantic sheer structure rises from the brick pavers like scaffolding over the existing east and west wings. The steep roof, slipped down and as compressed as a vertical wall, leans against the historic pavilion like a haphazard prop, a tiltup left unfinished for a lunch break. It seals off the pavilion's inner court, exemplifying the add-on possibilities of frame construction identified by Sigfried Giedion in *Space, Time, and Architecture*.[3] Here, the modernist legacy of structural transparency becomes elided with the rhetoric of wireframe axonometrics and the later notational transformations of structure prioritized in early digital design. Anticipated by Peter Eisenman's balsa wood–frame model for the Emory Performing Arts Center featured on the cover of the Greg Lynn–edited 1993 issue of *Architectural Design*, "Folding in Architecture," this is a frame tradition passed on to Andersen and Preissner, both progeny of the first digital generation, via Lynn at the University of California, Los Angeles (Andersen), and Columbia University (Preissner). Later clues and manifestations of this ongoing inquiry into the frame were provided by others of the first digital generation, notably Stan Allen in his research on the balloon frame and his domestic proposal for the 2017 Chicago Architecture Biennial. In the case of Andersen and Preissner, the addition is everything the existing pavilion is not: in mass (open versus solid), material (wood versus marble and bricks), texture (rough versus smooth), color (beige versus pink and white), profile (tall and narrow versus low and wide), duration (temporary versus permanent), and aperture (continuously striated versus episodically punched). The project is an X-ray, a section as much as a facade, a thick drawing and a flat construction at the same time. The placement and constitution of the project not only consign the historic pavilion to mere silhouette, a recessive shadow behind a structure made of lines, but cancel out the overleveraged category of "pavilion" entirely. By integrating the existing building into a new whole, the addition sends up architecture's recent pavilionization. It is the ultimate un-pavilion.

Second, the project registers as a fragment. The north elevation, sans eaves with lopped-off dormers, suggests an excision from a longer structure. The east and west elevations, more accurately cross-sections, reveal a four-story A-frame split in half—a cropped cabin, escapist chalet, and ski lodge rolled into one. The long, narrow plan suggests a severed tetra-level veranda. Whichever way it is looked at, the fragment channels Giedion's second observation on America's wood-frame house: it can be "cut down" and "moved to a

---

3   Sigfried Giedion, *Space, Time, and Architecture*, 4th ed. (Cambridge, MA: Harvard University Press, 1963), 361 (e.g., "addition of wings"; "new roof spread over all these additions").

new site."[4] Andersen and Preissner simulate such severing and mobility. Yet at the same time, their fragment is less found object than distillation. Purified in profile and detail, it is a customized artifact: exaggerated proportionally in section (less than 10 feet at its widest point; more than 40 feet in height), the half A-frame avoids an off-the-shelf look.[5] Deprived of standard door and window openings, and therefore lacking headers and double studs, it is purged of irregularities. With simplified dormers—reduced here to notational equilateral triangles—the roof plane acquires a sense of caricature. Now perfectly aligned in stud, joist, and rafter, every plane—roof, floor, wall—becomes unified in a monomaterial, monotonal oneness. Contrary to the casualness of everyday wood-frame construction, Andersen and Preissner's fragment is deliberate, measured, and exact. It eschews the sentimental reverence of frame construction exhibited in Otherothers's 2017 Offset House, in Sydney. It avoids the shattering of the box manifested in Frank Gehry's 1977 Santa Monica house addition. And it steers clear of the formal accumulation expressed in Rudolph Schindler's 1934 Bennati Cabin, at Lake Arrowhead, California. Instead, the fragment condenses common bits of Americana into what once, in that vague interlude between Deconstructivism and the digital, might have been called a "weak form"—a form so precisely low in definition that it could assume multiple identities while confirming none of them.[6] As a multifarious vernacular, the fragment finally *Americanizes* the US Pavilion in ways that forcefully contradict Trump's (now cancelled) order "Promoting Beautiful Federal Civic Architecture."[7]

Third, the project is all front: a tall, narrow, flat relief positioned before a low, wide volume. While the proportions recall those of Pezo Von Ellrichshausen's freestanding wood-framed Mine Pavilion for Denver's 2013 Biennial of the Americas, the juxtaposition of the project to the existing US Pavilion evokes the association with a Las Vegas billboard to its casino, a Western movie facade to its set, Eugenio Galdieri's 1957 Metro Drive-In movie screen to its tile-clad box,[8] and perhaps most directly, Robert Venturi's 1967 "bill-ding-board" to its vaulted gallery for the National Football Hall of Fame at Rutgers University. Like Venturi's project, Andersen and Preissner's is "big in size but economical in cubage,"

---

4 Giedion, 361–62.
5 Many off-the-shelf A-frames are defined by an equilateral triangle in section. While common floor-to-rafter angles can range from 60 degrees to 72 degrees, Andersen and Preissner's exceeds the steeper angle. The largest off-the-shelf A-frame on the market appears to be Avrame's TRIO 150, at 15 meters long, 9 meters wide, and 8.75 meters high. Andersen and Preissner's half A-frame is almost double the length (27 meters long), narrower, and taller. For standard A-frame dimensions, see "A-Frame House Plans," Avrame, accessed August 3, 2021, https://avrame.com/tips/a-frame-house-plans and "How to Build an A-Frame," *Mother Earth News*, November 25, 2011, https://www.motherearthnews.com/diy/buildings/how-to-build-an-a-frame-ze0z1111zhir.
6 Jeff Kipnis, "A Matter of Respect," *Architecture and Urbanism*, no. 232 (January 1990): 135. In another, more recent register, "weak form" may have some resonance with Bill Brown's attempts to recuperate the strangeness of "things" from their reduction to mere objects or commodities, arguing for a practice that "shows how a banal object (indeed, the fragment of an object) can become another thing." Bill Brown, *Other Things* (Chicago: University of Chicago Press, 2015), 46. This affiliation puts the work on display in the exhibition, and Andersen and Preissner's savvy choice of a fragment of a banal object or commodity-form, in a new light: playing the frame as a way to liberate the strange from the habitual.
7 See Elizabeth Blair, "President Biden Revokes Trump's Controversial Classical Architecture Order," NPR, February 25, 2021, https://www.npr.org/2021/02/25/971312635/president-biden-revokes-trumps-controversial-classical-architecture-order.
8 For an excellent account of this project see Davide Spina, "Il Drive-In," *AA Files*, no. 74 (2017): 173–82.

packed with "catwalks" and accessed by an axial entrance at the center of the facade.[9] But the quotations stop there. At 9 feet, 6 inches wide, 87 feet, 6 inches long, and nearly 41 feet high, Andersen and Preissner's structure is around a third of the size of Venturi's—the scale of a wood-framed house, not a football field.[10] Indeed, minus a couple of bays in length, it would almost fit inside the allowable buildable envelope of a standard 25-foot-wide by 125-foot-long Chicago lot (and with some imagination could be repurposed into an elegant home for one). Furthermore, by refacing the Palladian entry—its symmetry, pediment, columns, rotunda—with a suburban facade, Andersen and Preissner invert the front-to-back nature of Venturi and Denise Scott Brown's "decorated shed." Inverting VSB's rhetorical front with conventional behind, Andersen and Preissner's project instead puts a *conventional front* on the existing pavilion that houses the exhibition's now *rhetorical behind*: that is, the historical, technical, and social documentation of wood-frame construction. By extension, a curatorial decision transforms the US Pavilion into a nominal shed. A back-of-house building for a behind-the-scenes exhibition.

Fourth, the project is both prologue and epilogue, literally that which is both *before* and *in addition* to the word (or, per Rowe, *morale*). In plan, the structure establishes the beginning and end of an exhibition narrative that passes from familiar examples to ethereal atmospheres, serving as entry and exit. As the tail that wags a giant speech bubble circulation diagram, it first channels visitors into an exhibition loop through its center, directing them into the US Pavilion via an entry on the left-hand side of the courtyard. From here, visitors pass through a U-shaped sequence of galleries that exhibit, consecutively, photographs of construction sites, wooden models of generic houses, photographs of construction workers, wooden models of mobile homes, cottages for those displaced by natural disaster, and a doghouse, and, finally, atmospheric black-and-white photographs of trees and people. Upon exiting the galleries on the right-hand side of the courtyard, visitors are once again confronted by the four-story structure, which this time reads as an abstracted backstage curtain through which they will pass back onto the Giardini's stage, through its center. As prologue, the structure "introduces the world of wood framing as directly as possible allowing people to experience its spaces, forms, and techniques firsthand."[11] Serving as an exhibited artifact, it opens the story about wood frames and establishes a material context for sight, touch, and smell without offering any information about the exhibition inside. As epilogue, the project flaunts the possibilities of wood-frame construction as Architecture. While everyone might live in a frame, not every A-frame is an Architecture-frame. As beginning and end, the project spatializes and materializes a narrative at an architectural scale.[12] It is a display put to work. And all in good, clean fun.

Fifth, the project is of the great outdoors, or what Reyner Banham once referred to as "America's monumental space."[13] It establishes two types of open-air rooms. First are the elegantly long verandas stacked inside. At grade, the veranda is entered on central axis from the Giardini forecourt, or on cross-axis at each end. The space has all the continuity, visual

9   Robert Venturi, "A Bill-Ding-Board Involving Movies, Relics and Space," *Forum* 128 (April 1968): 74–79.
10   Venturi's Hall of Fame screen is 100 feet high and 210 feet long.
11   Paul Andersen and Paul Preissner, "U.S. Pavilion Commissioners' Statement," 2019.
12   See, for example, Martin Puryear's open-work architectural screen for *Liberty/Libertà, Swallowed Sun (Monstrance and Volute)*, installed in front of the US Pavilion in 2019, and Estudio Teddy Cruz's print *60 linear mile section San Diego/Tijuana*, installed in the same location in 2008.
13   Reyner Banham, "A Home Is Not a House," *Art in America* 53, no. 2 (April 1965): 73.

flow, and breezy informality of a Hawaiian lanai. Above, three more verandas of decreasing floor width are stacked in section, and accessed from stairs at the east and west sides. The verandas float between the existing tree canopies like layers in a dislocated treehouse. Accessorized with commissioned furniture by Norman Kelley (eclectic rocking chairs and other Shaker-inspired seats), they offer views back toward Venice and outdoor living rooms. Second, the project defines an exterior patio, furnished with four long, exquisitely varied wood benches designed by Ania Jaworska, straight from her urban-garden oeuvre for vacant lots in Chicago. Together, veranda and patio, striped in shadow and light, imbued with the odor of untreated wood, creaking underfoot, and furnished with hand-crafted chairs and benches, manifest as a space of leisure, at once boardwalk and jungle gym, a direct counterpoint to the work and labor depicted (and practiced) inside. Furthermore, it refutes Banham's claim that "from the Cape Cod cottage, through the balloon frame" Americans "do not monumentalize or make architecture."[14] By doing it all, the project unifies and at the same time deformalizes the existing pavilion by association.[15]

Finally, the project provides spectacle. For into this monument to the great outdoors, this space of leisure, enter tourists who unwittingly reenact images of behind-the-scenes labor. In a Disney-like simulation of the real, figures populate the frame like neighbors in a barn-raising scene.[16] One can easily imagine the selfies that mimic photographs of construction workers on the job. One can also imagine other scenarios, inspired by those staged by Charles and Ray Eames: couples posing in the frame as if it's a Case Study House; collective lineups between rafters in a giant "People Wall," à la the IBM pavilion at the 1964 New York world's fair. Whichever way the performances are carried out, the populating of the frame offers one last novelty: it's not just that everyone inhabits a frame, but that anyone can perform inside one. If Frank Gehry's skeletal wood-frame facade for the *Strada Novissima* at the 1980 Venice Architecture Biennale polemically critiqued historicist postmodern facadism by offering the frame as something to *look through*,[17] Andersen and Preissner's vernacular structure critiques a certain kind of elite formalism by providing the opportunity to play inside. As a 1:1 dollhouse, the project offers a "vernacular spectacular," an "Absolute Fake," a frame that is better than reality.[18] It suggests a blank canvas awaiting animation, a stage set pending reenactments.

In all these ways, the project reasserts design as the primary lens through which to view architecture's behind-the-scenes activities. By adding, distilling, scaling, integrating, accessorizing, and populating space, form, and structure, the frame becomes architecture.

14 Banham, 73.
15 Andersen and Preissner achieved a similar deformalization in their installation *Five Rooms*, for the Landmark Gallery of the Chicago Cultural Center at the 2017 Chicago Architecture Biennial, *Make New History*. There, five new stepped walls, clad in glossy brown tiles, introduced the everyday aesthetic of public schools and swimming pools into the decorative grandeur of the existing cultural center. The effect of this interior rehab was to turn a grand public piece of architecture into a more casual, recreational one.
16 A scene recently enacted by Assemble in photographs of their Yardhouse project under construction.
17 Germano Celant, *Artforum*, December 1980: "In the end the most radical intervention is decidedly that of Frank Gehry, the California architect, who has refuted monumentalizations and imitations by proposing a wood-frame skeleton through which to view the 16th-century architecture of the arsenal 'in perspective,' thus turning this post-modernist rebirth into what might be called a 'renaissance of the Renaissance.'"
18 See Wouter Vanstiphout, "Vernacular Spectacular," *hunch*, no. 8 (Summer 2004): 48–51, and Umberto Eco, *Travels in Hyperreality*, trans. William Weaver (San Diego: Harcourt Brace Jovanovich, 1986).

If *morale* serves as a Trojan horse for *American Framing*—the "inside" content serving to smuggle in a contraband "outside"—in the end, it is physique that triumphs. No doubt some will find this privileging of form off the mark and indulgent. But, as Arthur Drexler wrote of an earlier generation, in *Five Architects*: "An alternative to political romance is to be an architect, for those who actually have the necessary talent for architecture. The young men represented here have that talent (along with a social conscience and a considerable awareness of what is going on in the world around them) their work makes a modest claim: it is only architecture, not the salvation of man and the redemption of the earth. For those who like architecture that is no mean thing."[19] Indeed, as *morale* continues to serve as a cover for business ideals—collaboration, innovation, nichification, etc.—its ideological argument abandoned for "impact," *physique* prevails exactly at the moment when it needs to.

At the same time, the surprising message that Andersen and Preissner's project delivers is the fact that wood-frame construction is not just the same something for everyone in the American context, but is the same something for everyone everywhere. Its conceptual and material malleability has captured the imagination of architects all over. Given its ubiquity, one cannot help but wonder if there is something else at play in *American Framing*: namely, a subconscious desire to retrieve (or is it rescue?) a degree of American *exceptionalism* in the frame after its global dissemination. Into this landscape, Andersen and Preissner offer an architecture of the highest (and lowest) order: an architecture that asserts design as a front-stage activity; an architecture that situates the architectural object into a network of photographs, commissioned furniture, and scale models; an architecture indebted to and embedded within the historical project that it transforms; an architecture that upgrades vernacular construction into uniqueness; an architecture that relegates the existing US (né European) Pavilion to a nominal shed; an architecture that begins and ends with the outside; an architecture that offers subversive performances; an architecture that elevates the prosaic and destabilizes the formal; an Architecture *Americana*.

---

19   Arthur Drexler, "Preface," in *Five Architects*, 1.

How Framing Works
Paul Preissner

Real estate has a different purpose than architecture: it exists to satisfy the requirements of the owner (and sometimes user), and more importantly, it is a place to park money. If you're going to buy something to park money in, then you do so needing to know that you will at some point find a buyer so you can withdraw your money (ideally with ridiculous profit). Once you decide that your interests in architecture include the ability to withdraw your money from it, then all your concerns about architecture as a practical art and how it works (or looks) are conceded to this future buyer; you're living in someone else's house. Since your future buyer is only imaginary until the future, then it follows that all those other aspects you might be concerned with have to be the least problematic or unattractive (in every sense) to the most possible people so that your future buyer might actually exist.

In the essay "Toward a Critique of Architectural Ideology" (1969), Manfredo Tafuri identifies the plan as the organizer of space, which orders society, and as a result produces the ideological purpose for the entire enterprise of architecture. The essay traces the migration from the plan as the project of the architect (and therefore architecture) to the plan as the project of the city. Up until recently, he argues, the city developed largely planless, and as a result the city (and therefore society) was conditioned by architecture, whereas in the modern capitalist endeavor, the city (and its plan) began to move architecture from its position as an ideological subject into a materialist object, effectively neutering the political force that architecture (through the plan) could provide. In this evacuation of architectural purpose toward society, and the role of the avant-gardes in hastening the organization of the plan into the plan of capitalist development, Tafuri finds reason to accuse architecture of accepting its commodification and relinquishing its responsibilities as a subject (and being operative).[1] This new role of architecture and the architect produced an anxiety that was resolved through a change in the priorities of architecture, privileging the function of delight and novelty. Architecture, which once conditioned the city, became conditioned by the city, and because the city was no longer the planless accumulation of architectural subjects but now ordered by the plan of development (and capital), architecture serves only to create novelty.

Theodor Adorno explored a similar issue in art in *Aesthetic Theory* (1970), where he expresses an ambivalence to the role of novelty in art. While commending efforts to move away from the totalizing aesthetics of universality, he criticized the fetishization of newness and production of novelty as mimicking the logic of capital, and therefore being complicit with the exact forces it is supposedly attempting to negate. In this regard, the role of architecture in modernity—to generate novelty—seems entirely similar to the role of art in its performances of superficiality in order to meet the demands of capital, and its satisfaction to be the surface and the producer of superficiality. This happens, but it's not the only outcome of architecture's redefinition as real estate. Tafuri describes the efforts to recover the lost subjectivity of architecture through the pursuit of "authenticity":

1 Architecture was "the first discipline to accept…the consequences of its already realized commodification…. Modern architecture, as a whole, was able to create…an ideological climate for fully integrating design, at all levels, into a comprehensive Project aimed at the reorganization of production, distribution and consumption within the capitalist city." Manfredo Tafuri, "Toward a Critique of Architectural Ideology," in *Architecture Theory since 1968*, ed. K. Michael Hays (Cambridge, MA: MIT Press, 2000), 14.

> The problem is that now the only way left in the search for the authentic is the search for the eccentric.[2]

To struggle with its new role as a consumed object, architecture turns to novelty in order to reaffirm its significance in the world.

Both Adorno and Tafuri acknowledge the difficulty of cultural practice in the age of capital, and, in a way, their critiques of art and architecture, respectively, are just depressing explanations of our contemporary conditions. The conditions of capital and the development plan of the city subject architecture into a kind of weakened state of existence, recognized for its presence more than its action, or the action of its presences instead of the operation of its order—the plan having been utterly dissolved in favor of expression. The crushing reality of this situation is that the same modern technology that architecture (and the architect) imagines as useful in producing subversion (which it misunderstands to be shocking novelty) does little more than reinforce the same structure that rendered architecture without societal power in the first place: novelty is chased, sometimes produced, mildly disrupts societal sensibilities, is commodified, and then is reproduced in variation until it manages to produce merely a ¯_(ツ)_/¯; by then hopefully some other new novelty has been discovered. On and on. Work by those looking to change the attentions and priorities of society as it exists gets swallowed into the same condition of being an object in the city rather than a subject, and as a result, reinforce it no differently than those happy with the status quo.

This is the existence of architecture as an object and not a subject, of architecture as real estate. The misconception is that this situation pushes architectural choices to only the blandest, the most "beige"—an idea that presumes architecture to be a practice of finishes. In practice this desire to be able to sell produces both blandness and novelty (to be bland enough not to offend imaginary future buyers, or novel enough to delight imaginary future buyers). Which is to say it now primarily appeals to taste in one way or the other. The trouble with taste is that it appeals to class, and further subjects architecture to being conditioned by the city, rather than conditioning it.[3]

Whether novel or bland, both trajectories of architecture have conceded any consequential difficulty. The eccentricity or inoffensiveness supported by today's imaginary future buyer is entirely superficial, residing only in the visual and not in the ordering aspects of architecture. Architecture as an object can be anything or nothing and look like whatever it wants (eccentric or ordinary) as long as it's not difficult. Being difficult requires people to make more complicated choices, and to reexamine priorities, expectations, and assumptions about the world.

This (difficulty) was the political power of architecture before capitalism, and has become problematic as a quality of architecture during capitalism. Its purpose, to appeal to the tastes of imaginary future buyers, can handle a full spectrum of superficialities, but has absolutely no room for upsetting priors in any deep way. Architecture as an object needs to be liked or disliked. This simple relationship is a solid requirement for consumer products, of which architecture is now one. Difficulty in architecture produces a deep anxiety that the imaginary future buyer will always be just that, never materializing, and never allowing one to withdraw money from ~~architecture~~ real estate.

2   Tafuri, 16.
3   I wrote about this in *Kind of Boring* (New York: Actar, 2021).

This is what it means to have surrendered the plan and succumbed to being an object rather than a subject in the world: complete participation in the world of taste.

Whether you think this is a problem or not, I suppose, depends on whether you think the role of architecture (or art) is to reexamine the world, which involves being difficult, or to cheerfully continue it as is; whether you think architecture should produce some type of reflection accessible to everyone equally, or whether you think it should be entertaining and collectable and indicate taste (or class). If you want an architecture that feels more meaningful than its utility as a place to park money, then it's worth considering an alternative to the exploration of architectural eccentricity and ordinariness. If both approaches produce genres of architecture entirely susceptible (and more likely, that lend themselves) to being commodified, an alternative would be something that has the ability to more deeply affect, or disturb, expectations about a building, a form of architecture that challenges assumptions about use or appropriateness. Since the imaginary future buyer could come from anywhere, and in fact now comes from everywhere, this anxiety in architecture encourages universality and immediate recognizability: either something *Novel!* or something decidedly un-novel, but "tasteful." Ignoring those demands might make space for vernacular and idiosyncratic work, as a kind of veto on the development plan of the city. The trap to be avoided is trafficking in architectural style, or believing that architecture is about style at all, instead of working with plan, and instead exploring a more forceful and less controllable form of creativity where, rather than eventually domesticating the exotic through normalizing and commodifying what is eccentric, or trading in the well-known through maintaining normalcy, the normal is made weird. In order to do this, architecture might be thought of less as a thing (or an object) that's produced, and more as a form of creativity that examines space for an individual or groups of individuals, requiring more idiosyncrasy, more intuitions and personal preferences, and weirder propositions about how one might organize social space and private space, producing as a result an architecture that is inherently more difficult to understand, less accommodating to assumptions, and more challenging to the cities it resides in; becoming, again, a subject in the world, and not an object of it.

Difficulty in architecture, or difficult architecture, isn't the same thing as illegibility in architecture or illegible architecture (although sometimes it is illegible). To produce difficult work is to create something that questions existing assumptions about utility, use, appropriateness, politeness, societal morals, concepts of being neighborly, protection of the individual or exposure of the public, what people are asked to do with their time, the nature of labor and the origins of the materials, mythologies of privacy, the politics of domesticity, or the true nature of work and employment, among other things. If the architecture of capitalism requires smoothness and virtuoso complexity and tasteful anonymity and efficiency and thoughtful planning, resulting in something you can like, the characteristics of a difficult architecture should stand in the way of those qualities: it should be rough, dumb, outside taste, clumsy, resulting in confusion.

America in the early nineteenth century was undergoing a rapid expansion in both population (from immigration and births) and land (from a belief in Manifest Destiny), and needed a form of architecture not reliant on the European methods of building the colonialists brought over: masonry, heavy timber, etc. The logistics of population growth and settler occupation made traditional methods requiring skilled labor and slow work impractical.

Softwood framing originated as a kind of outside solution, one that came about through the simultaneous existence of plentiful and cheap wood ignored by carpenters and timber builders, small, light, and portable pieces of lumber, and cheap nails that could connect framing elements without skillful joinery. Where slow-growth, heavy timber is capable of carrying significant loads through massive beams and columns, softwood framing just calls for more weak wood, multiplying columns to make any individual column meaningless and creating something that has neither the structural clarity of a timber column nor the brute force of the masonry wall: the stud wall. The mobility of the 2×4 and ease of wood-frame construction allowed new people to produce architecture, and as a result, to produce space. At roughly the same time that architecture launched the search for novelty as the new pursuit of the architect, wood framing came along to allow architecture by non-architects, kept immune from the pressures of practice by simply not practicing, more interested in the idiosyncrasies of their own quotidian needs. This de-skilled labor initiated an architecture that eventually came to constitute over 90 percent of built housing in the United States.[4] It's this fundamental sameness that paradoxically underlies the American culture of individuality, unifying all superficial differences, organizing the irrelevant differences in finish that identify tastes. In this way, framing suggests an alternative to the narcissism of architecture open to its own commodification.

At the same time, framing introduces an improvisational creativity seemingly open to all other forms of creative practice, but generally unavailable to architecture. After all, architecture is planned, then drawn, then organized for construction, then built. There's no ability to move a wall on-site when building with prefabricated steel or engineered reinforced concrete. Framing doesn't require the same uptight approach to architecture. Lumber arrives on-site and is cut in place to do whatever. It's easy. Windows and doors can be introduced and removed at will. Walls can be moved or removed with little consequence, or consequences that a few more articles of lumber can resolve in no time. Wood framing allows for immediate and intuitive changes, accommodating desires unknown until realization. Framing is the closest architecture to action painting, a term introduced by the critic Harold Rosenberg to describe the postwar American approach to painting that let in-the-moment hunches direct process, producing work whose value isn't dependent on anything external.[5] But it's the more practical aspects of action painting that exist in framing that make framing consequential. The ability to change direction during construction without much effect on delivery time or cost allows for a medium of space that is vastly more mutable, wily, un-precious, and open to idiosyncratic experimentation that satisfies specific individual desires and curiosities. Framing allows architecture to be irrational, risky, and ugly, to make mistakes, creating space that stands in contrast to the industrialization of culture. It's this constant uncertainty and allowance during its production, its existential impermanence, that develops a space for creativity and architecture that resists the trend toward taste and solidity.

About one and a half billion years ago animal and plant lineages split.[6] This split eventually resulted in both trees and people, which still share nearly a quarter of genes, despite our separate journeys. In this essential way, we are closer to wood than to nearly every other

---

4   "Highlights of Annual 2020 Characteristics of New Housing," United States Census Bureau, accessed January 20, 2022, https://www.census.gov/construction/chars/highlights.html.
5   Harold Rosenberg, "The American Action Painters," *Art News*, December 1952, 22–23, 48–50.
6   See Daniel Y.-C. Wang, Sudhir Kumar, and S. Blair Hedges, "Divergence Time Estimates for the Early History of Animal Phyla and the Origin of Plants, Animals and Fungi", *Proceedings of the Royal Society B: Biological Sciences* 266, no. 1415 (January 22, 1999): 163–71, https://doi.org/10.1098/rspb.1999.0617.

building material. While we domesticate forests through row planting and grid harvesting, producing abstraction in the natural, forests reciprocally naturalize the abstraction that is architecture into a landscape of studs and temporary bracing and shims and incidental layouts made possible by the disorderly freedom of wood framing. Subversion can occur where the economic stakes of experimentation are so low that personal, anti-market desires and the unfashionable can be materialized, and normal things altered toward idiosyncrasy. Pressures from the development plan moved architecture to pursue expensive novelty or ordinary tastefulness in order to appeal to the imagined desires of future owners, trading away the future. Framing gets around this pressure through allowing for an architecture that can be impulsive and at times even gross—the result of ad hoc choices—without the consequences (change it again!). This introduces a liberatory creative freedom to architecture traditionally only found in other (cheaper and more immediate) forms of artistic practice.

The typical costs of architecture (labor, material, land, time) continually work against architecture's ability to explore impulse, and instead condition it to be deeply considered and planned. The loss of impulsive acts relegates architecture to a practice of conservatism, where everything is premeditated, designed for some sort of optimal someone who doesn't yet exist, always as a response to something and never an act of something. Framing works through crudeness; it's easy, it's cheap, everyone can learn it, and anyone can do it. Framing works by allowing for participation at every level and offering a way to act out architecturally, indulging instinct, accommodating ideas, and seeing where things land.

Acknowledgements

American Framing began as an idea to explore the world of the normal in architecture through the study of the most common and original form of American architecture: the wood-framed house. The project was first developed at the School of Architecture at the University of Illinois Chicago in 2018 and 2019, when we submitted it for consideration to represent the United States at the 17th International Exhibition of Architecture – La Biennale di Venezia. The exhibition appeared at the Biennale from May through November 2021. In 2022, versions of the exhibition traveled to Galerie Jaroslava Fragnera, in Prague, and Wrightwood 659, in Chicago, and in 2023 it was exhibited at the Palm Springs Art Museum. This book includes much of what was presented in the exhibitions, but expands that work to consider the history, context, and values that have shaped the way America approaches architecture.

American Framing would not exist without the enthusiasm, support, and criticism of many people.

First, we cannot find enough words to thank the students who formed the research and design team that produced the models for the exhibition, whose curiosity, rigor, and inventiveness gave the project its character: Emory Alba, Kassandra Alvarez, Alondra Ayala, Hannah Bernas, Kenda Blanks, Sama Jafarnejad Chaghoshi, M. Lorenze Cordova, Nathan Gawlinski, Ronald Hall, Esau Hernandez, Summer Hofford, Andrew Hunt, Andrew Huss, Jeffri Jacobe, Colin Jecha, Nash Kennedy, Tina Kracke, Riley Kyrouac, Sohui Lee, Shamsedin Mokber, Courtney Moushi, Martin Murungi, Kayla Oliver, Yamileth Ovalle, Jacob Patnode, Morgan Peterson, Sam Piombino, Meghan Quigley, Mallory Rabeneck, Rizna Rafi Maalouf, Ricardo Sandoval, Jocelyn Schneider, Cody Schueller, Martina Smith, Lia Thompson, Julia Turner, Giselle Valle Figueroa, Luna Vital Gallego, Andreina Yepez, and Roya Zanjani.

Daniel, Chris, Ania, and Carrie and Thomas, you were the most gracious collaborators we could have asked for. Thank you.

We are grateful to Walter Benn Michaels for helping with the initial project approvals from the University of Illinois Chicago, and to Rebecca Rugg for expanding that support with a level of enthusiasm and conviction that we could not have ever imagined. Limitless thanks are due to Judith De Jong and Adriann Anderson, who navigated a tangled mess of budgets, deadlines, and administrative miscellany to keep everything going. Bob Somol and the School of Architecture gave the project its intellectual home—thank you.

Without the guidance and comfort of Chiara Barbieri, we are not sure any of this would have worked out. There was a big wooden thing in Venice that will forever owe its existence to the otherworldly patience and attention of Giacomo Di Thiene.

We are grateful to Park Books for their generosity.

Finally, we are forever in the debt of our sponsors, whose support literally made the project real: the Bureau of Educational and Cultural Affairs of the United States Department of State; the National Endowment for the Arts; the University of Illinois Chicago; Glen-Gery Corporation / Brickworks; Alphawood Foundation; the Graham Foundation for Advanced Studies in the Fine Arts; Architectural Record; Joseph and Mary Burns; Brooklyn PrintWorks; HDR; and the Thornton Tomasetti Foundation.

Biographies

Pablo Alvarado is the founder and co-executive director of the National Day Laborer Organizing Network. Harold Meyerson is editor at large of *The American Prospect*.

Paul Andersen is an architect and principal of the Denver-based practice Independent Architecture. He is clinical associate professor of architecture at the University of Illinois Chicago and the author of *The Architecture of Patterns* and *The Monuments Power the Cars*.

Catherine Caufield is an author whose writing and activism focus on the environment.

Penelope Dean is professor of architecture at the University of Illinois Chicago and the founding editor of *Flat Out*.

Joe Gilmore is a graphic designer and educator based in York, in the United Kingdom.

Dan Handel is an architect and curator. He is the editor of the publications *Aircraft Carrier*, *Yasky and Co.*, and *Manifest: A Journal of American Architecture and Urbanism*.

Rebecca Gayle Howell is the poetry editor of the *Oxford American* and the author of two novels-in-verse, *American Purgatory* and *Render*.

Ania Jaworska is an architect and educator. She is clinical assistant professor of architecture at the University of Illinois Chicago and principal of Associates Associates.

Jayne Kelley is an editor and writer. She is clinical assistant professor of architecture at the University of Illinois Chicago, a co-editor of *The Museum Is Not Enough*, and a co-author of *The Western Town*.

Thomas Kelley and Carrie Norman are principals of Norman Kelley, a practice based in Chicago and Cambridge, Massachusetts.

Adam Kotsko is an American theologian, religious scholar, culture critic, and translator working in the field of political theology. He is the author of *Why We Love Sociopaths*, *Awkwardness*, and *Žižek and Theology*.

Stephen H. Norwood is professor of history at the University of Oklahoma.

Paul Preissner is an architect and principal of Paul Preissner Architects. He is professor of architecture at the University of Illinois Chicago and the author of *Kind of Boring*.

Daniel Shea is an artist based in New York City working in the mediums of photography, installation, and sculpture.

Chris Strong is a photographer and videographer based in Chicago.

Ernest Wilkins is a Chicago-based writer and entrepreneur. He is the social marketing lead for social audio at Twitter.

Imprint

Concept
Paul Andersen, Jayne Kelley,
Paul Preissner

Copy editing, proofreading,
and rights and reproductions
Jayne Kelley

Graphic design
Joe Gilmore

Image processing, printing,
and binding
Druckerei Kettler, Bönen/
Westphalia, Germany

Publication © 2023 University of
Illinois Chicago; Paul Andersen,
Jayne Kelley, and Paul Preissner;
and Park Books AG, Zurich

Installation photographs on
pages 80-85, 99, and 105
© Stefano Graziani
All other installation and model
photographs courtesy of
American Framing

See image caption pages for
additional source and copyright
information. The editors have
made every effort to identify and
contact owners of copyright. We
apologize for any mistakes or
omissions and ask that copyright
owners notify the publisher of
these oversights, which will be
corrected in future editions.

Excerpt from "Bogalusa
Burning" © Southern Historical
Association. Reprinted courtesy
of the *Journal of Southern
History*.

Excerpt from "The Ancient
Forest" © Catherine Caufield,
1990. Reprinted by permission
of the author.

Excerpt from "Helping the
Powerless Build Power,
Pablo Alvarado: An Oral
History" by Harold Meyerson
© *The American Prospect*,
Prospect.org, 2021. Reprinted
by permission of *The American
Prospect*. All rights reserved.

All other texts © the authors

Park Books
Niederdorfstrasse 54
8001 Zurich
Switzerland
www.park-books.com

Park Books is being supported by
the Federal Office of Culture with
a general subsidy for the years
2021–24.

All rights reserved; no part of this
publication may be reproduced,
stored in a retrieval system or
transmitted in any form or by any
means, electronic, mechanical,
photocopying, recording, or
otherwise, without the prior
written consent of the publisher.

ISBN 978-3-03860-195-1

Image captions

p. 236 top
John Young. Illustrations of trees: *Abies douglasii* (Douglas fir), *Abies menziesii* (Sitka spruce), and *Abies williamsonii* (mountain hemlock), published in *U.S.P.R.R. Exp. & Surveys-Cal. & Oregon*, ca. 1855. Yale Collection of Western Americana, Beinecke Rare Book and Manuscript Library, Yale University

p. 236 bottom
Darius Kinsey, photographer. *On the spring boards and in the undercut – Washington bolt cutter and daughters*. Near Seattle, Washington, ca. 1905. Prints and Photographs Division, Library of Congress. Public domain

p. 238 top
A rendering of live cladoxylopsid trees, the first trees, which emerged approximately 380 million years ago. Peter Giesen, illustrator. Courtesy of Peter Giesen

p. 238 bottom
A view of a saw mill and block house upon Fort Anne Creek, the property of Genl. Skeene, which on Genl. Burgoyne's army advancing, was set fire to, by the Americans, published in Thomas Anburey, *Travels through the Interior Parts of America. In a Series of Letters* (London: Lane, 1789). Emmet Collection of Manuscripts Etc. Relating to American History, The New York Public Library

p. 239
Armin Elmendorf. Patent drawing of oriented strand board (OSB), from patent no. 3,164,511, issued 1965. United States Patent and Trademark Office. Public domain

p. 240 top left
Laziz Hamani, photographer. Cartier Juste un clou ring, 2012. © Laziz Hamani

p. 240 top right
Steve Greenberg. *Spotted Owl: Don't Blame Me*. Editorial cartoon published in the *Seattle Post-Intelligencer*, 1993. © Steve Greenberg

p. 240 bottom
C. R. Clark, photographer. Burnt District Coffee House, Chicago, from a book of photographs taken before and after the Chicago Fire, approximately 1865–72, 1911. Courtesy of the Newberry Library

p. 241 top
Diagram of wall framing with platform construction, from L. O. Anderson and O. C. Heyer, *Wood-Frame House Construction, Agriculture Handbook* no. 73, United States Department of Agriculture, 1955. Public domain

p. 241 bottom
Richard Scarry. Excerpt(s) and illustrations from *Richard Scarry's What Do People Do All Day?*, 1968. © Richard Scarry, 1968; renewed 1996 by Richard Scarry II. Used by permission of Random House Children's Books, a division of Penguin Random House LLC. All rights reserved

p. 242
Illustration of common nails, date and publisher unknown

p. 243
Patent drawings of nailing tools. Top left: S. Anderson, hammer, from patent no. 4,155, issued 1845; top right: G. F. Voight, hammer, from patent no. 712,983, issued 1902; bottom left: M. Pearson, nailing tool, from patent no. 876,086, issued 1908; bottom right: M. B. Smith et al., nail gun, from patent no. 2,648,841, issued 1953. United States Patent and Trademark Office. Public domain

p. 244
J. L. Ollig et al., patent drawing of nail gun, from patent no. 2,927,324, issued 1960. United States Patent and Trademark Office. Public domain

p. 246 top
"Hacksaw" Jim Duggan, date unknown. WWE. Fair use

p. 246 bottom
Scene of lumberjack with child, published by the Western Art Association, Chicago, 1873. LC-DIG-ppmsca-59492, Prints & Photographs Division, Library of Congress. Public domain

p. 247
Cover of *Physique Pictorial* vol. 16, no. 2, by Bob Mizer, with illustration by Tom of Finland, April 1967. Courtesy of and under license by Bob Mizer Foundation

p. 249 top left
Fred Sandback. *Untitled*, 1967. Photostat, 8 ½ × 11 in (21.5 × 27.9 cm). Fred Sandback Archive

p. 249 bottom
Fred Sandback's studio at Yale School of Art and Architecture, New Haven, 1967. Fred Sandback Archive

p. 249 top right, 250
Frank L. Baum, author, and W. W. Denslow, illustrator. Pages from *The Wonderful Wizard of Oz* (Chicago: G.M. Hill, 1900). Rare Book and Special Collections Division, Library of Congress. Public domain

As far as loggers, millworkers, and others in the timber industry are concerned, the issue is a simple one: jobs versus owls. The anger and fear of the threatened workers are reflected in the black humor of bumper stickers saying "SAVE A LOGGER, KILL AN OWL" and T-shirts emblazoned with the motto "I ♥ spotted owls...barbecued, fricasseed, baked, stir-fried." One mill-owner showed me a spotted-owl joke that had come through on his fax machine: "What's the difference between a spotted owl and a logger? A spotted owl can still make a small deposit on a new pickup."

The northern spotted owl lives only in Northern California, Oregon, and Washington, but it has become a symbol to timber workers everywhere who are fearful of losing their jobs. In imploring a Senate panel meeting in Sitka, Alaska, not to cancel the pulp mills' monopolies in the Tongass National Forest, John Parton, a logger for the Alaska Pulp Corporation, compared himself with the owl. "I, too, am an endangered species," he said. "I am ... a Pacific Northwest logger. Will you give my mate and I thousands of acres of timberland, for that is what I, too, need to survive." All through the Pacific Northwest, loggers and others in the timber industry are holding rallies, marches, and "spotted-owl barbecues"—often with their employers footing the bill—to protest the threat to their jobs.

The timber industry in the Northwest has been suffering for years, however. Its problems predate public concern about ancient forests or the spotted owl. Throughout the region, mills—especially mills that depend on big, old trees—have been closing down. Some towns, such as Westfir, Oregon, that were founded on timber and until recently thrived on it have lost all their mills. Oregon's Department of Employment has reported that between 1977 and 1987 the state lost more than twelve thousand jobs in logging and wood processing, and that its timber industry now provides only about five per cent of Oregon's jobs. As other industries—notably tourism, now No. 3 in Oregon—pick up the slack, timber is losing some of its political clout in the region. Nevertheless, David Mumper, a timberlands resource manager at Weyerhaeuser, recently said of Washington State's growing population, "I look at it as twenty thousand people a year moving into the state that have no use for us, because our industry's not growing. Politically, the people in this state could kill us."...

Right now, most old-growth wood is used wastefully: centuries-old Douglas firs are cut into two-by-fours and used to frame our houses; rare cedar planks are nailed into molds for poured concrete and then thrown away; ancient hemlocks are pulped and converted into rayon or cellophane, wrapping paper or disposable diapers. "That's just plain wrong," Bart Koehler, of the Southeast Alaska Conservation Council, says. "When a four-hundred-year-old tree ends up on some baby's ass, it's an insult to all that's good and right with the world."

Fast-growing, coarse grained, knotty wood from plantations can do many of the jobs now being done by wood from the ancient forests. But products that require high-quality wood—fine furniture, wooden boats, musical instruments, and more plebian objects, like door and window frames—will become luxury items or disappear altogether. "Composite materials will take the place of solid wood," William Banzhaf, of the Society of American Foresters, says.

Catherine Caufield
From "The Ancient Forest," *The New Yorker*, May 14, 1990

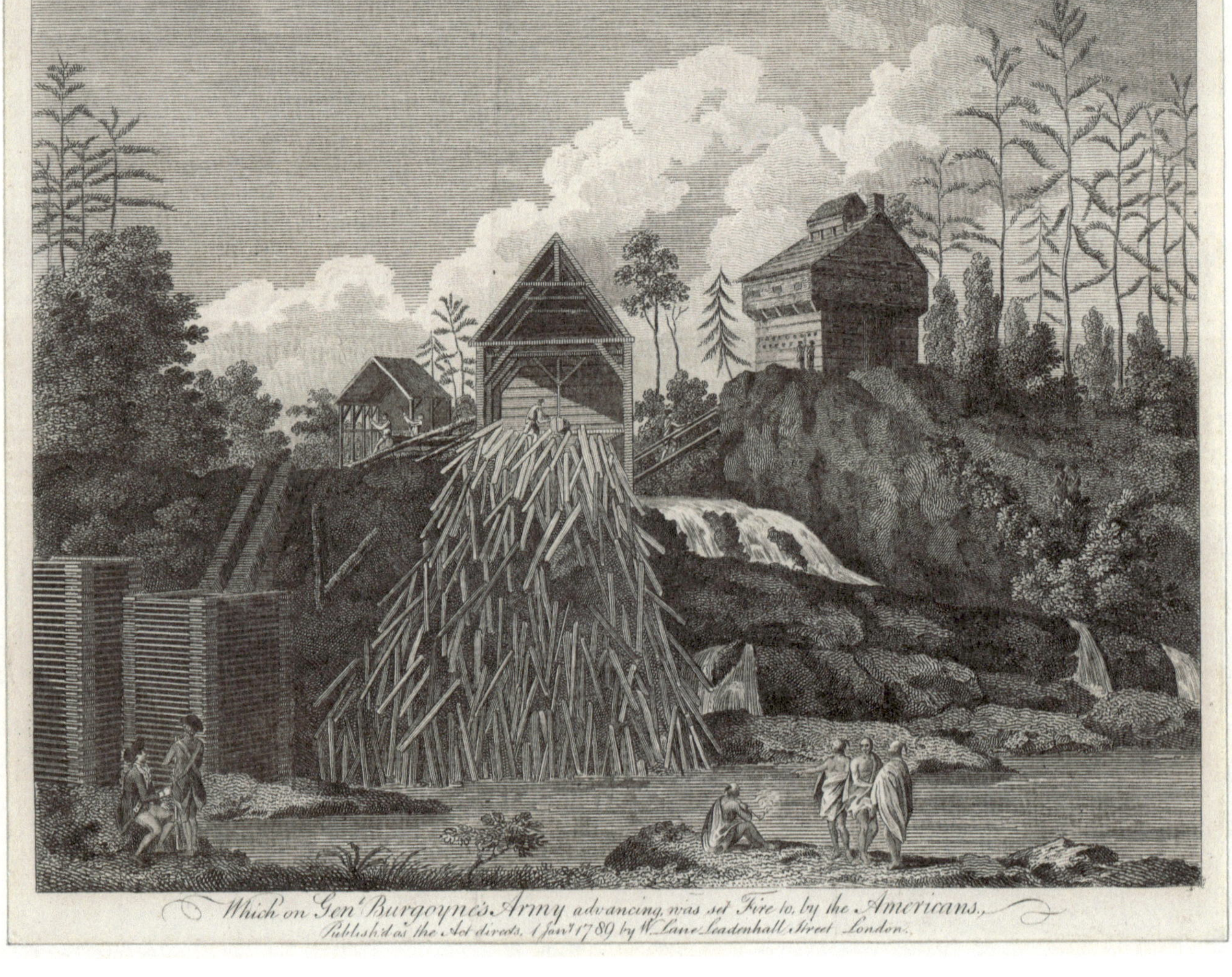

A View of a Saw Mill & Block House upon Fort Anne Creek the property of Genl Skeene.

Which on Genl Burgoyne's Army advancing, was set Fire to, by the Americans.
Publish'd as the Act directs, 1 Jany 1789 by W. Lane Leadenhall Street London.

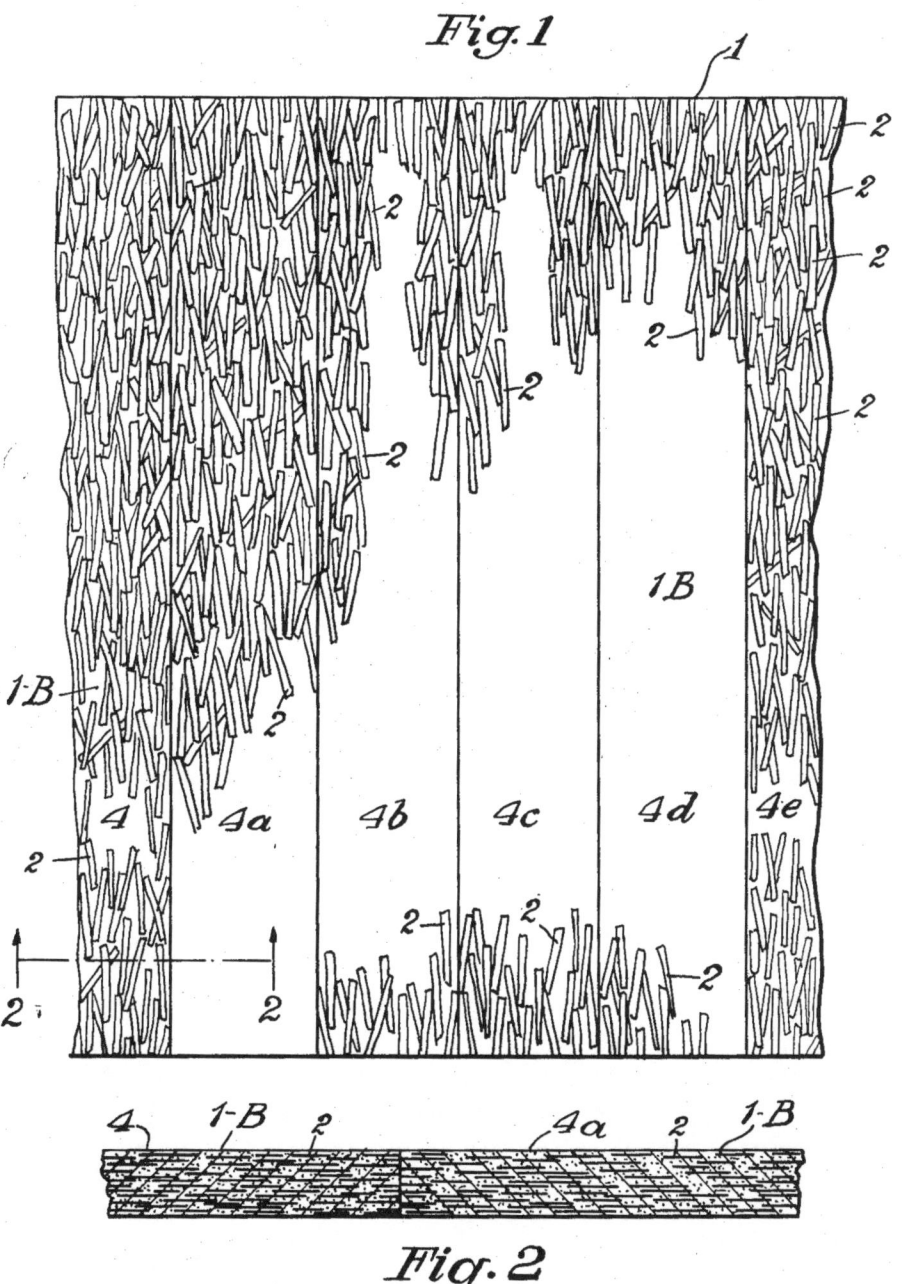

DON'T BLAME ME... I JUST LIVE HERE

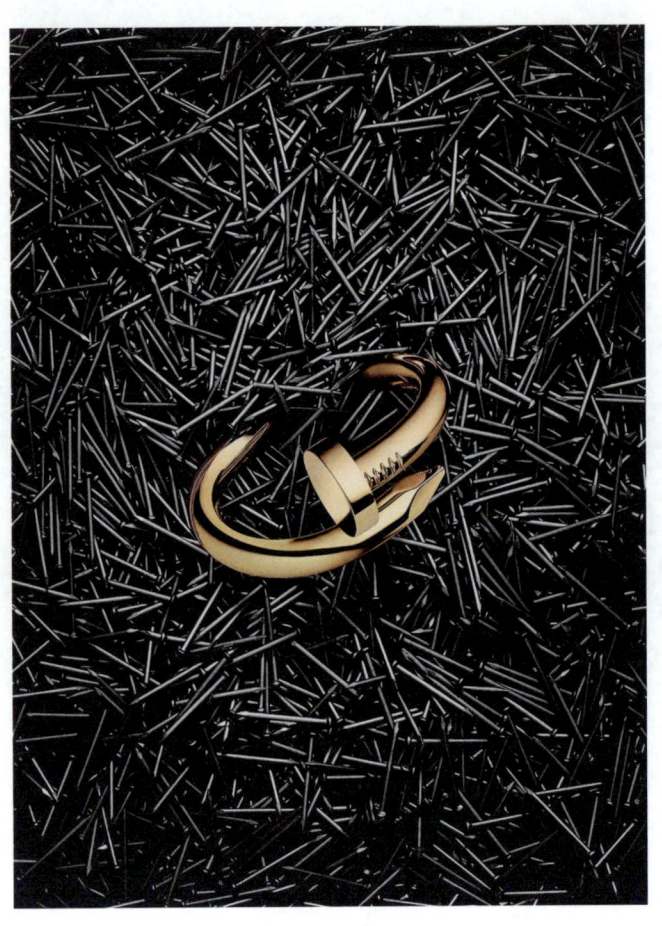

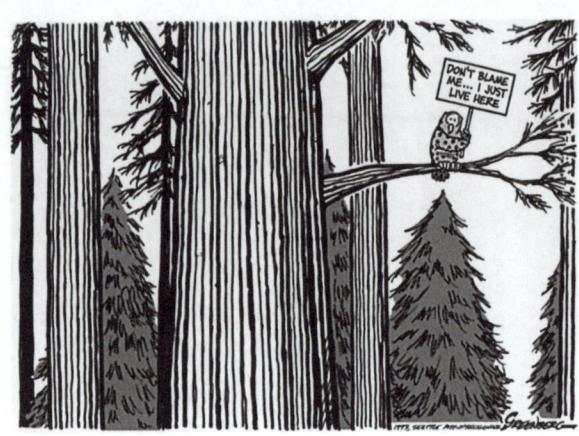

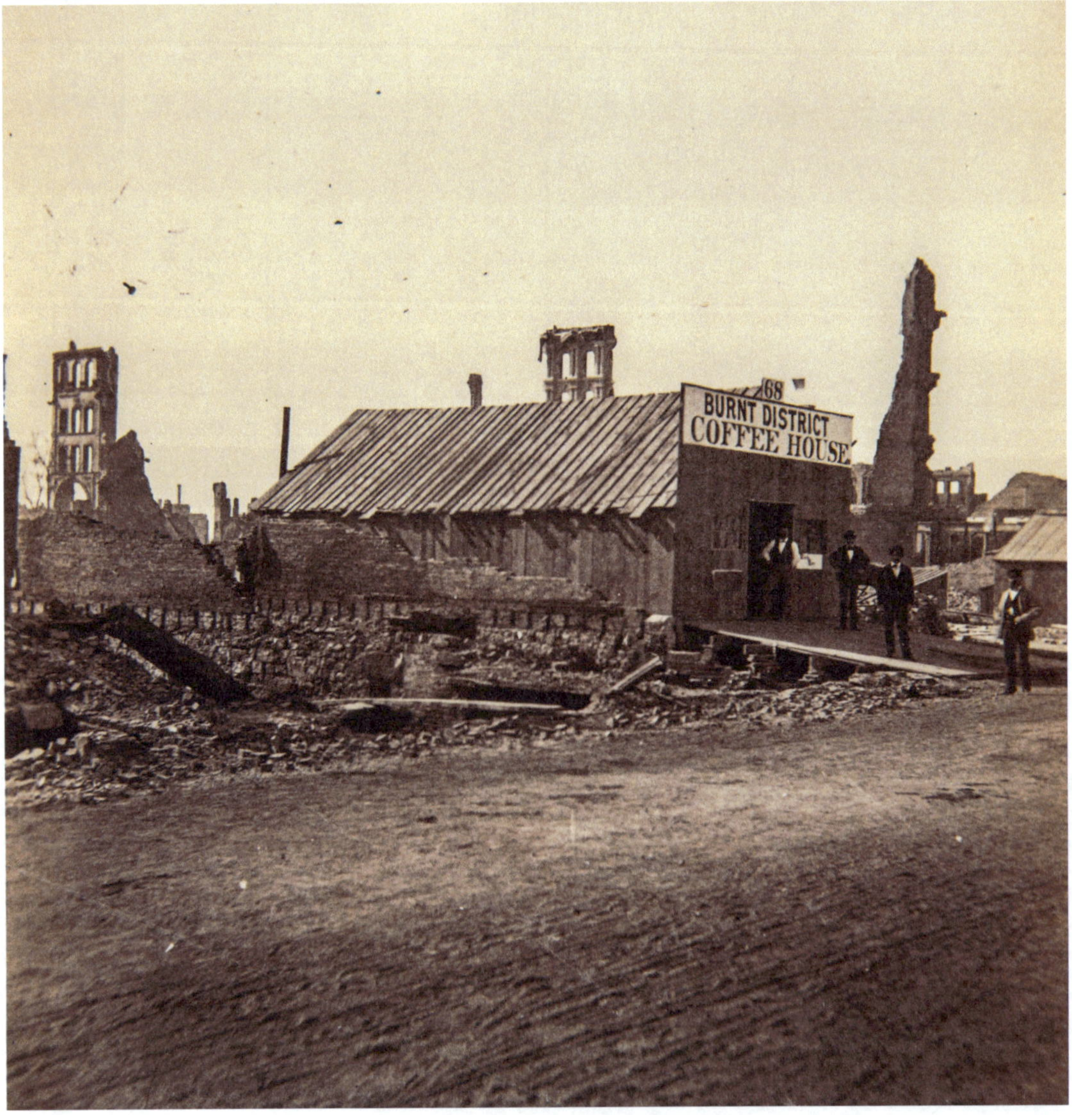

68
BURNT DISTRICT
COFFEE HOUSE

WOOD-FRAME HOUSE CONSTRUCTION 33

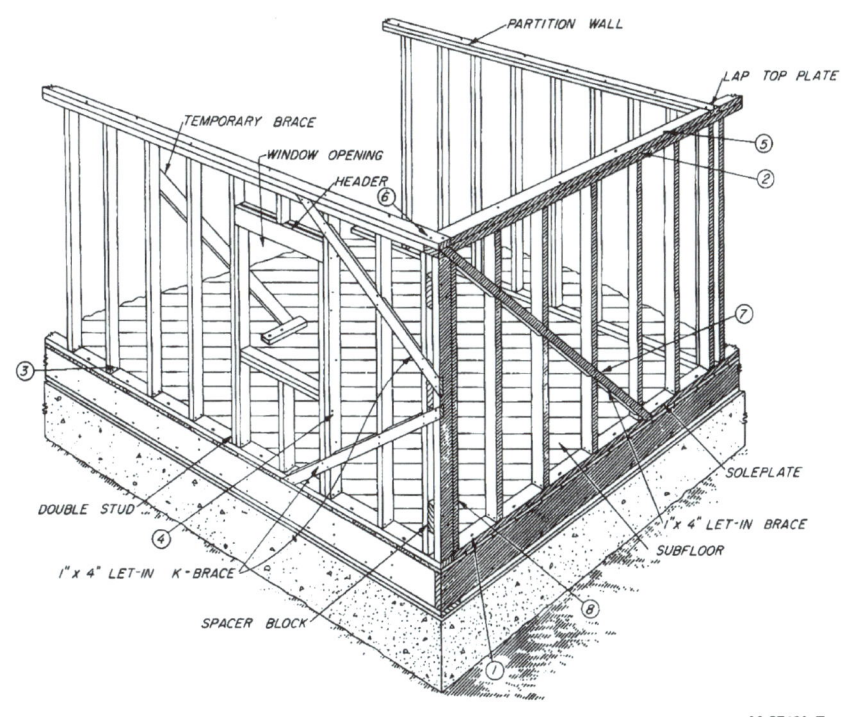

They put in water pipes.
They put in sinks and bathtubs and toilets.
They put in a furnace to keep the house warm.
They nailed down floors.
And Jason built the chimney higher.

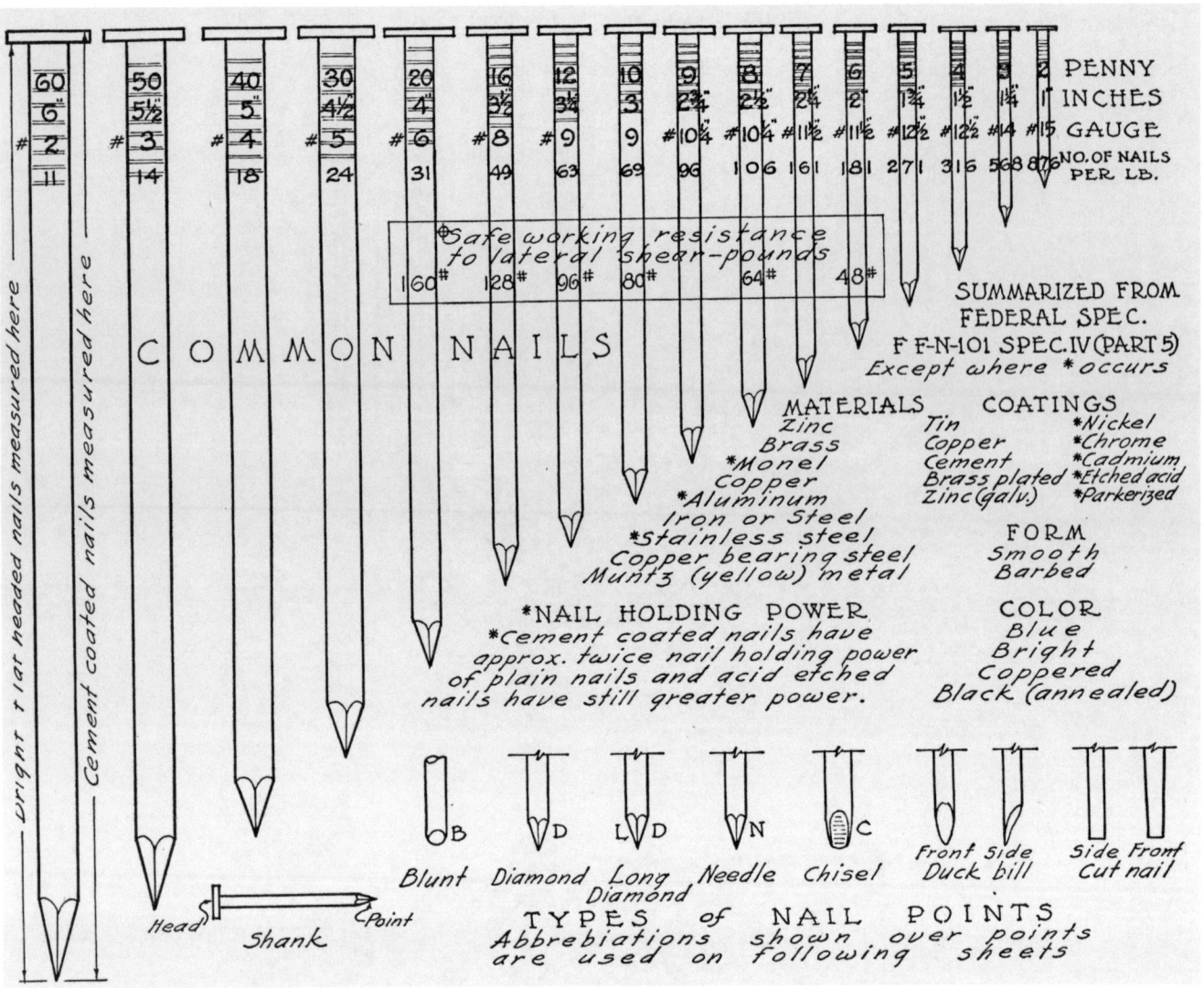

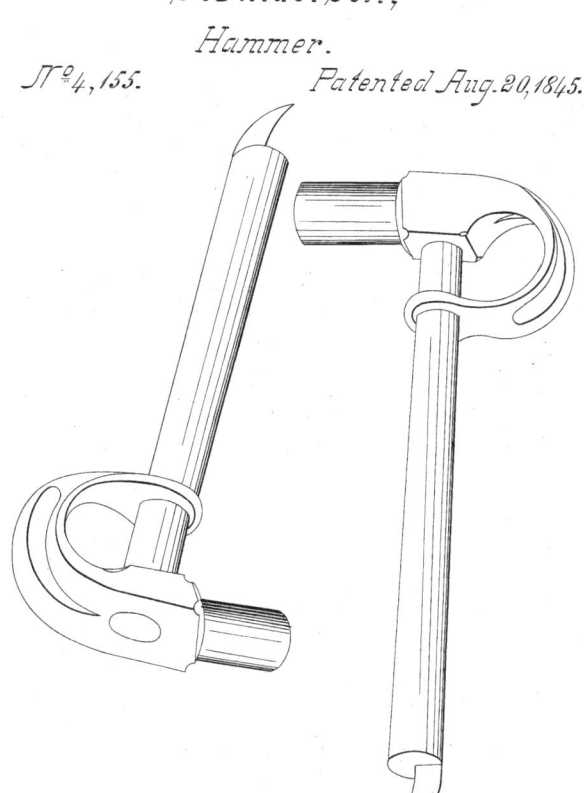
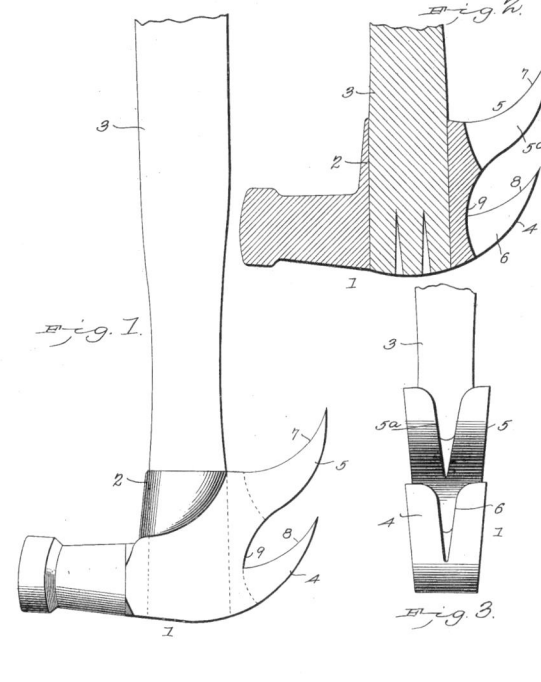
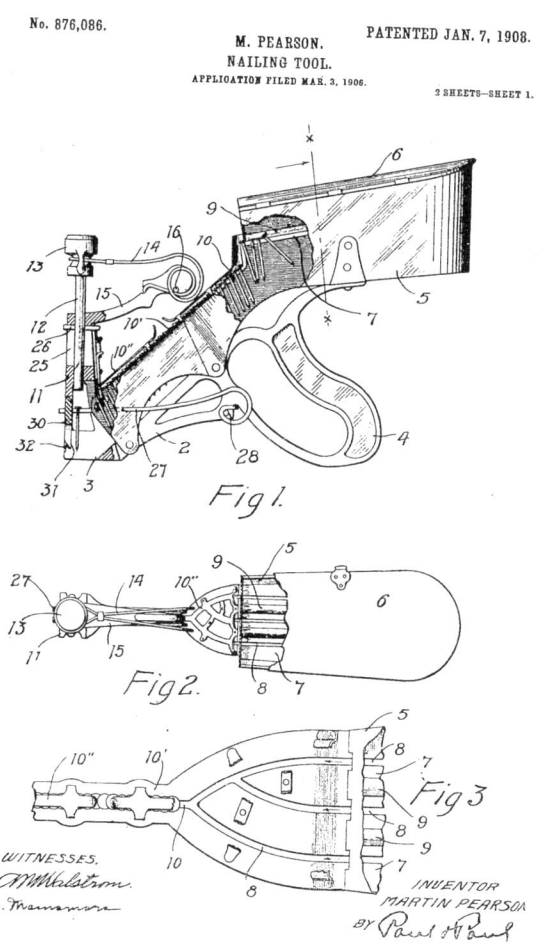
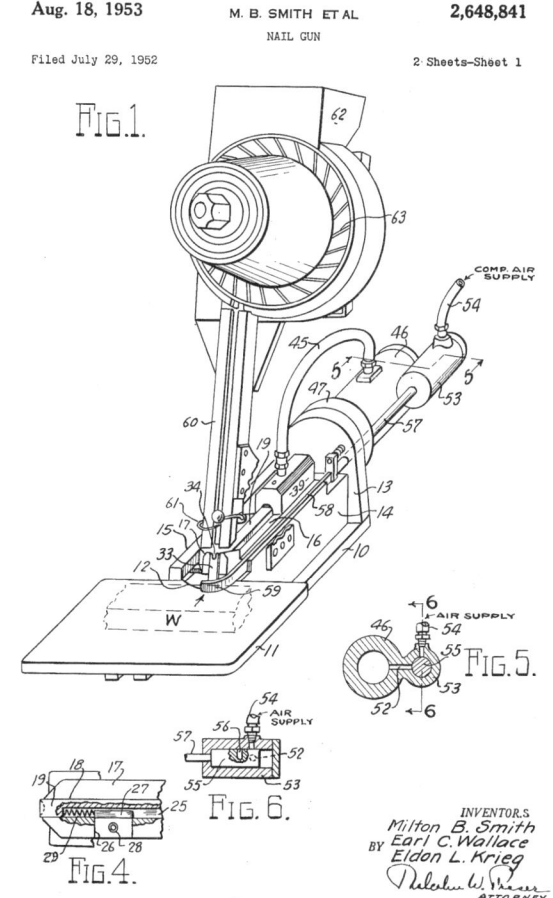

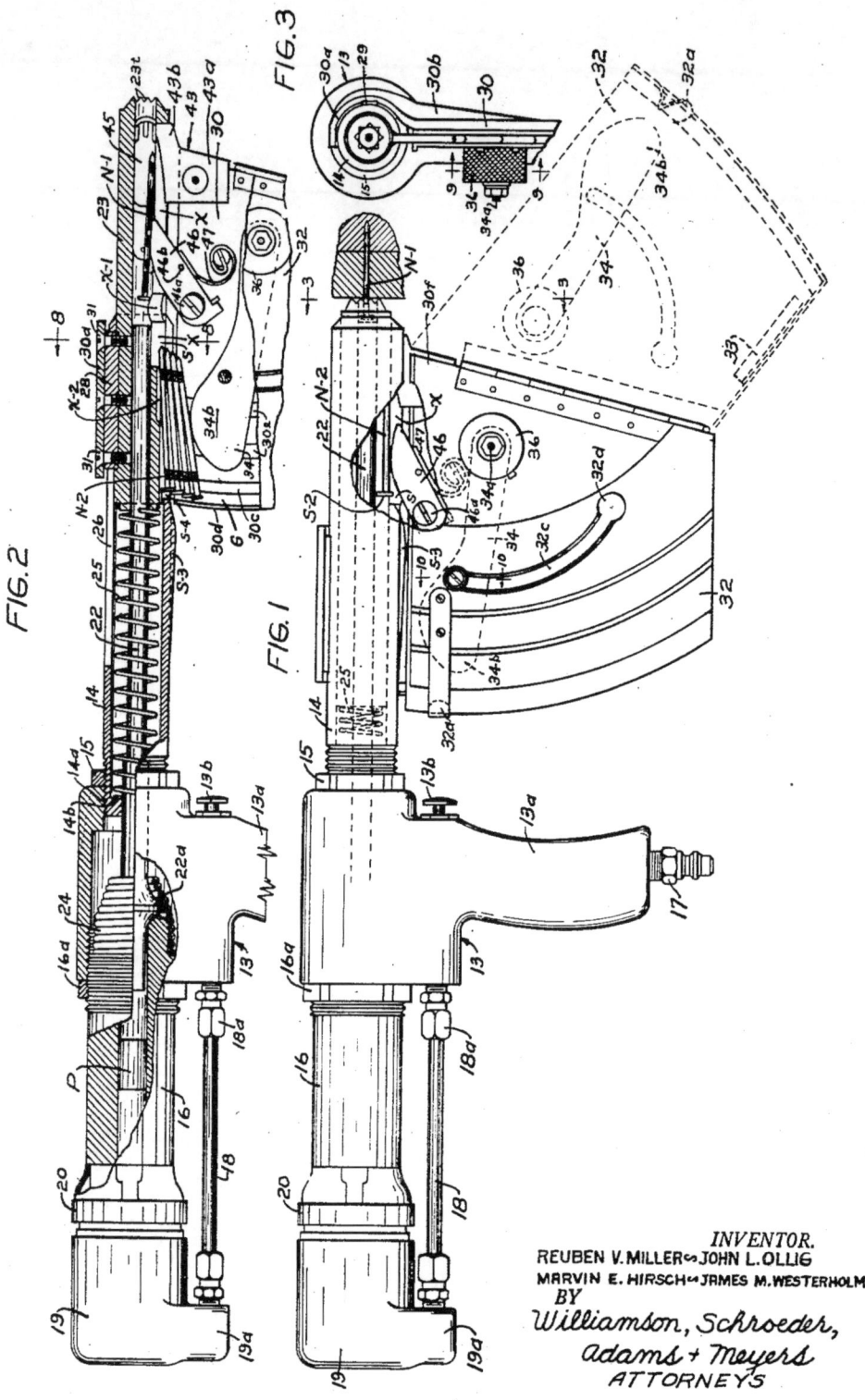

In January 1996, I was hired to run the day laborer organizing project by CHIRLA [the Coalition for Humane Immigrant Rights, based in Los Angeles]. I was a paid organizer, and I worked 16 hours a day because I loved what I was doing!

Day laborers were generally viewed as unorganizable, marginal workers, but we demonstrated otherwise. On many corners, they came to agreement to set wage standards for themselves, to reverse a process that had been a race to the bottom. I worked on enabling them just to keep working, just to have the right to assemble on corners to get work.

When I began working for CHIRLA, I would go to two particular street corners, both in front of HomeBase (now Home Depot) stores, that were patrolled by the L.A. County sheriffs. Tensions between the workers and merchants would often escalate to near-violence, the sheriffs would abuse their authority, and the stores would hire private security guards, some of them racists, who were abusive, too. Many people in the neighborhoods had preconceived notions about day laborers—that they were littering, loitering, drinking in public, and by their presence devaluing their property. That was the norm on many corners....

As cities tried to keep the workers off the sidewalks in the early 1990s, they began enacting anti–day laborer ordinances banning them from standing on sidewalks. We said it was a form of speech and assembly protected by the First Amendment. Between 1992 and 2012, we took 20 municipalities that had enacted such ordinances to court. We didn't just take them to court. Every time we sued a city, with did a march with our allies—that showed the police that we weren't alone in this. When we'd organize a corner, neighbors and merchants would come to meet with us. We'd look for local residents who were sympathetic, and to local civil rights groups. We'd build a coalition. We were building power for the historically marginalized.

Once hearings began, the workers filled the courtrooms. It was an education for them and for the judges, it put a human face on what was at stake.

We kept winning these cases. After a time, a number of cities, including Glendale, Burbank, and Pasadena, said they'd open a day laborer center and give us funds to run it, but they'd still ban the gatherings on street corners. In return, we had to agree not to sue them over their ordinance. We said no. We knew that poor people need options. If there's a day labor center, workers should go there voluntarily, not be brought there by the police, in handcuffs, because they were arrested for standing on a street corner. We challenged these cities in court, and won.

Pablo Alvarado
From "Helping the Powerless Build Power, Pablo Alvarado: An Oral History,"
by Harold Meyerson, *The American Prospect*, August 31, 2021

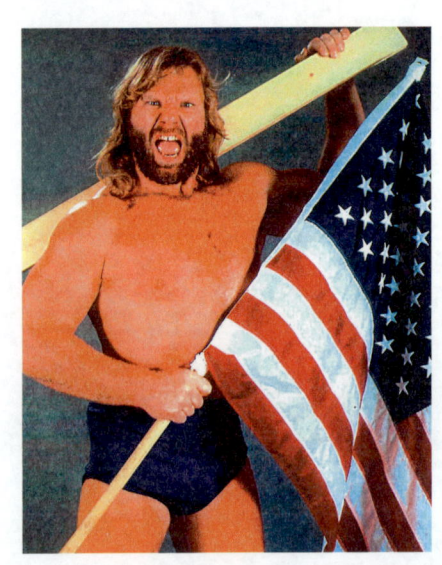

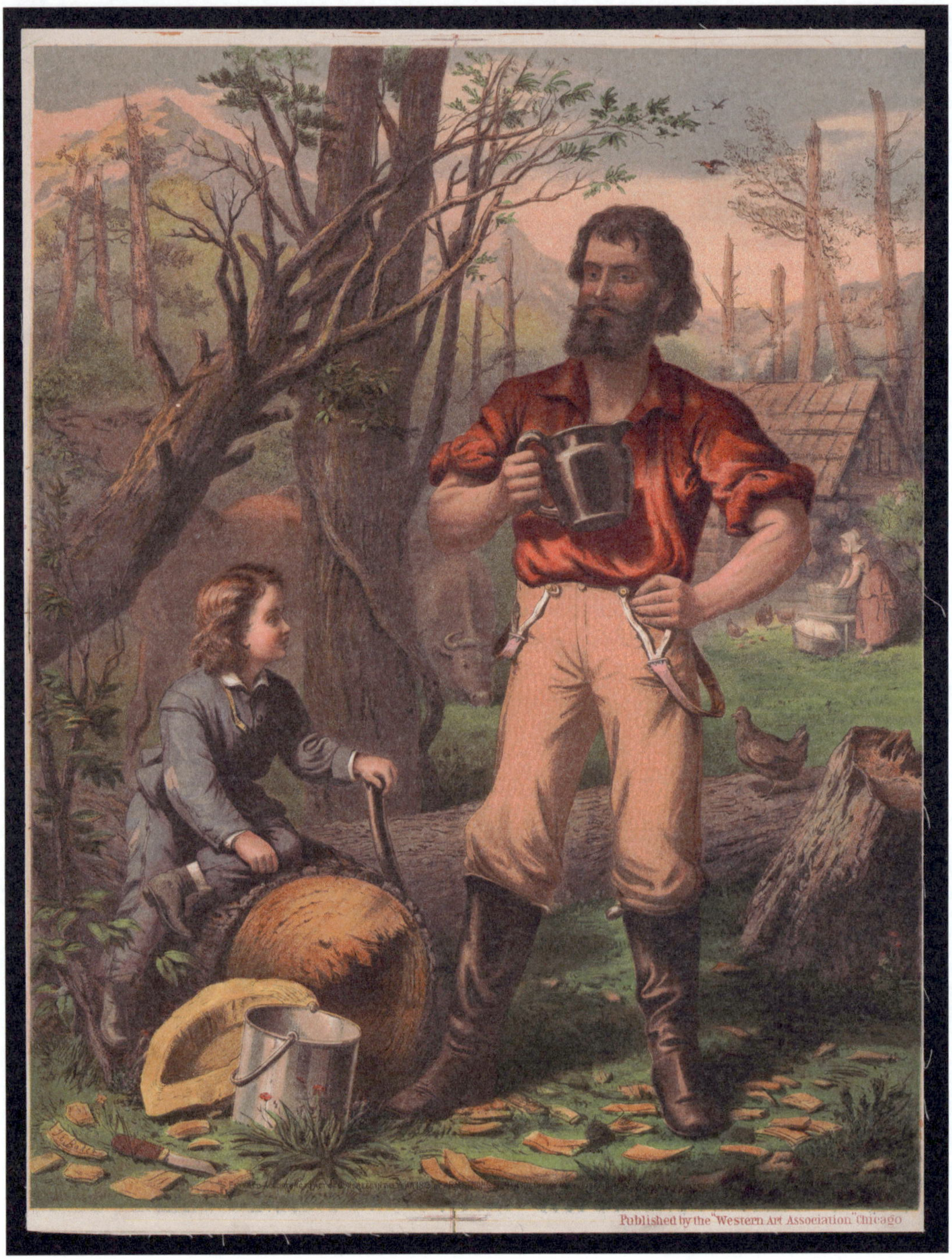
Published by the "Western Art Association" Chicago

If you were to give me a couple of cocktails, I could make the case that professional wrestling is one of the most important American cultural innovations ever created. It touches the highest rooms of power in this nation. Remember: the last guy to serve as President of the United States is a WWE Hall-of-Famer.

The early professional wrestling companies tailored their programming to their clientele. The competitors were larger-than-life representations of good, evil, and the nuance that lives between those two extremes. Some characters are metaphors for the everyman, the blue-collar, hard-workin' man the common American sees themselves as (or is assumed to).

Take "Hacksaw" Jim Duggan, for example. Duggan was a popular wrestler in the 1980s who won legions of fans with his time-honored gimmick of being an over-the-top patriot. Duggan's persona—a rough-and-tumble, lovable oaf who always clutched his trademark 2×4—was not unique or elaborate; therefore, he never needed to change it. His character never became tired or old to fans because it encapsulated what they loved about America: hard work, perseverance, and pride. If you need more proof that Hacksaw Jim Duggan is America incarnate, just look at him: he's got the body of every unathletic high school football player; he has the face of every small-town barroom brawler; he has a beard like every American lumberjack since Paul Bunyan carved out a nation from trees with his axe. He's just like us! Except maybe more patriotic, because he carries an American flag everywhere he goes.

During WrestleMania III—the 1987 edition of what is basically WWE's Super Bowl—Duggan staged an iconic moment that is still talked about today, during a match he wasn't even billed in. The fight got off to a heated start; the crowd was silenced to allow the foreign villain Nikolai Volkoff, who was teamed up with the Iron Sheik, to sing the Soviet national anthem. Out of nowhere, Duggan *sprints* down to the ring to stop him, armed with his trusty 2×4 (with a tiny American flag attached to it). Minutes later, when the heels have the good guys on the ropes, Duggan absolutely clobbers the Sheik; 93,000 people start chanting "U-S-A," to the point the walls start shaking. It is one of the most surreal moments in the history of American pop culture.

Ironically, Duggan's persona also represents the twilight of American industry. Despite winning the hearts of millions, he never held a major title as the "Hacksaw" in any of his companies. He's an athlete who wants nothing more than to prove himself, and though he's good at what he does, he will never be considered one of the greatest.

Duggan once said, "I think the character is just an extension of my personality. My old buddy Bret Hart always said, 'I'm the best there is, the best there was, and the best there ever will be.' I always say, 'I'm Hacksaw Duggan. I try hard.'"

Ernest Wilkins

Dorothy LIVED IN the midst of the great Kansas prairies, with Uncle Henry, who was a farmer, and Aunt Em, who was the farmer's wife. Their house was small, for the lumber to build it had to be carried by wagon many miles. There were four walls, a floor and a roof, which made one room; and this room contained a rusty looking cooking stove, a cupboard for the dishes, a table, three or four chairs, and the beds. Uncle

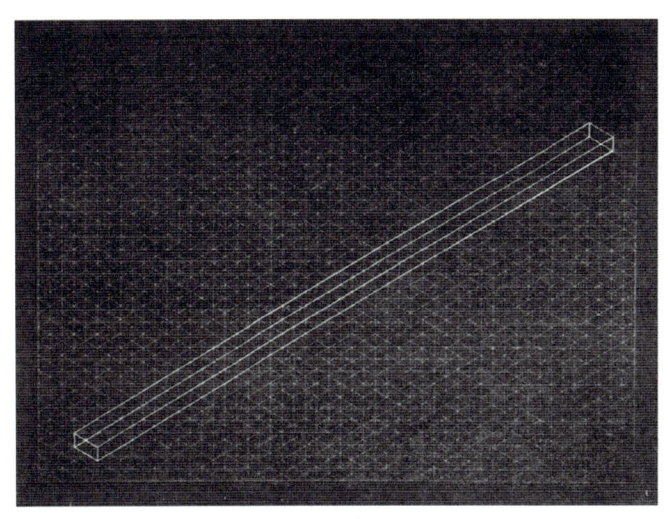

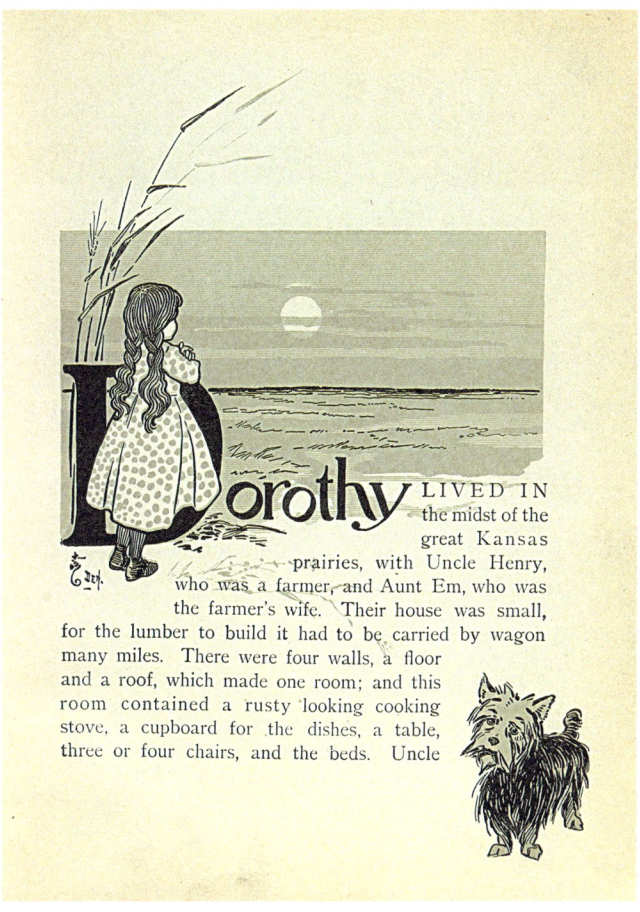

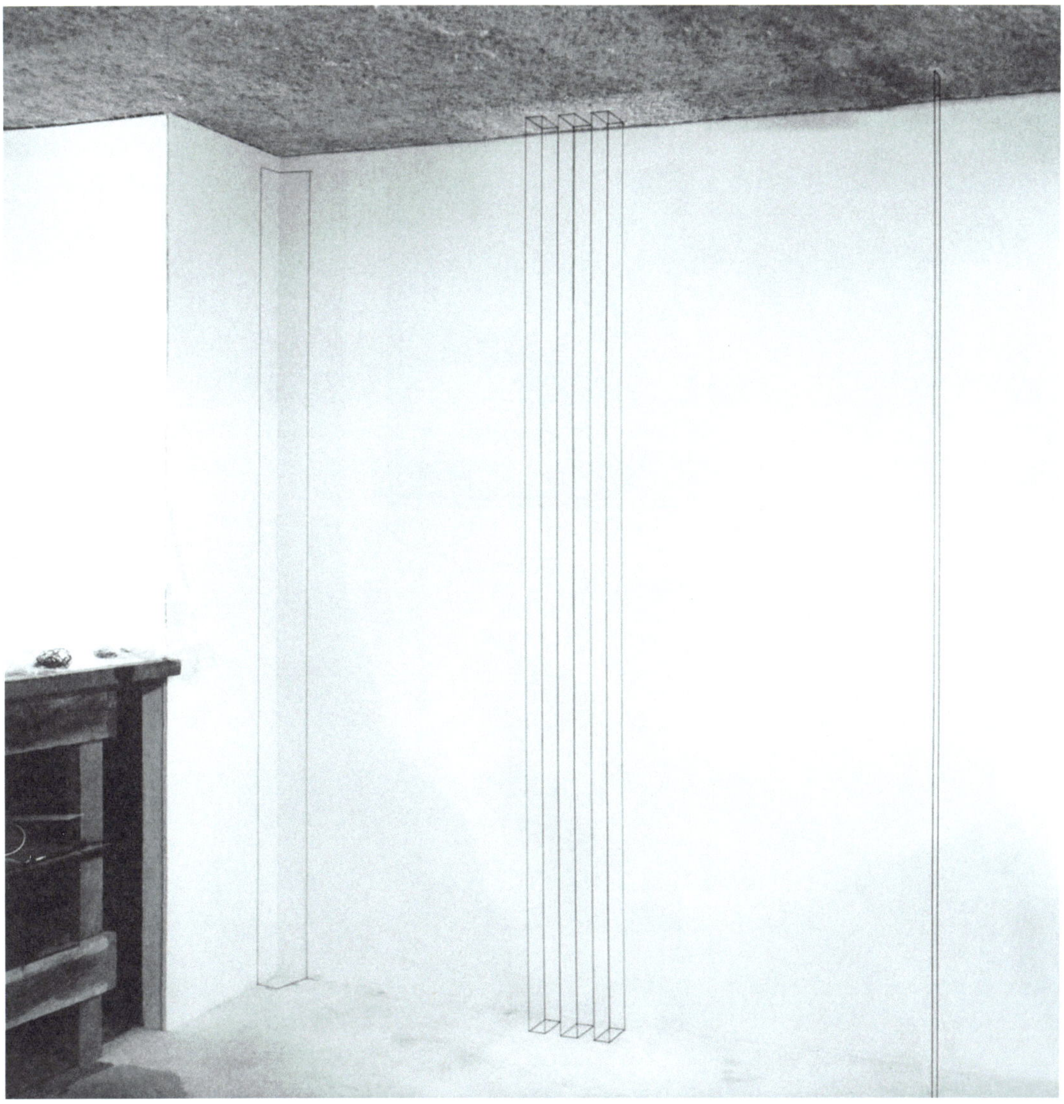

"She caught Toto by the ear."